U.S. Department of the Interior

Bureau of Land Management

RIPARIAN AREA MANAGEMENT

A Selected, Annotated Bibliography of Riparian Area Management

Technical Reference 1737-1

July 1987

RIPARIAN AREA MANAGEMENT

A SELECTED, ANNOTATED BIBLIOGRAPHY OF RIPARIAN
AREA MANAGEMENT

Compiled by Paul Cuplin
Edited by Raymond J. Boyd
Bureau of Land Management
Denver Service Center

INTRODUCTION

This Technical Reference, developed by the Riparian Area Management Task Force (1985-86), lists 135 references which the Task Force feels represent the most significant contributions from the over 1,200 references reviewed.

The bibliography is stored on the DPS-870 mainframe computer at the Bureau of Land Management, Denver Service Center. The bibliography can be copied and downloaded to a microcomputer for the addition of local site-specific references.

Anonymous. 1981. Developing strategies for rangeland management. A report prepared by the committee on developing strategies for rangeland management, Board on Agriculture and Renewable Resources, Commission on Natural Resources, National Research Council, Washington, DC. 91pp.

LOCATION: U.S.

KEYWORDS: LAND MANAGEMENT POLICY, FLPMA, INVENTORY, LAND USE PLANS.

ABSTRACT

The Federal Land Policy and Management Act of 1976 (FLPMA) established procedures for the development and protection of all lands in the public domain. Approximately 70 million ha (174 million acres) of such lands in the western United States are managed by the Bureau of Land Management (BLM) under principles of multiple use and sustained yield. BLM is required by FLPMA to make an inventory of the resources of these lands and to prepare comprehensive land use plans consistent with the management goals set forth in the act. In addition, BLM is required by the National Environmental Policy Act of 1969 to prepare environmental impact statements for major actions affecting the environment. The Bureau is now preparing these statements within their grazing management program.

Anonymous. 1982. The best management practices for the management and protection of western riparian stream ecosystems. Western Div. American Fisheries Society. 45pp.

LOCATION: WEST, U.S.

KEYWORDS: BEST MANAGEMENT PRACTICES

ABSTRACT

To provide guidelines applicable to riparian habitat fisheries, and water quality resources, the Western Division of the American Society has developed this paper listing Best Management Practices for the seven primary impacts of livestock grazing, mining, water development, irrigation, road construction, agriculture, urbanization, and timber harvest.

Almand, J.D., and W.B. Krohn. 1978. The position of the Bureau of Land Management on the protection and management of riparian ecosystems. Pages 359-361 in Strategies for Protection and Management of Floodplain Wetlands and Other Riparian Ecosystems. R.R. Johnson and J.F. McCormick, tech. coord. Proc. Symp. Dec. 11-13, 1978, Callaway Gardens, GA. U.S. Dep. Agric., For. Serv. Gen. Tech. Rep. WO-12 Wash. DC. 410pp.

LOCATION: U.S.

KEYWORDS: BLM POLICY

ABSTRACT

This paper discussed the Bureau of Land Management's policy and procedures for protection and management of riparian ecosystems. Past abuses of riparian habitats are recognized as are future opportunities for improved management. Recent legislative and executive mandates require land managers to protect the natural functions of riparian ecosystems. BLM is implementing a positive program to adequately protect and manage components of riparian ecosystems.

Anderson, B.W., and R.D. Ohmart. 1985. Managing vegetation and wildlife along the Colorado River: Synthesis of data, predictive models, and management. Pages 123-127 in Riparian Ecosystems and Their Management: Reconciling Conflicting Uses. Proceedings of the Symposium. US Dep. Agric. For. Serv. Gen. Tech. Rep. RM-120, 523pp. Rocky Mountain Forest and Range Experiment Station, Fort Collins, CO.

LOCATION: AZ

KEYWORDS: PREDICTIVE MODELS, WILDLIFE

ABSTRACT

Predictive models were developed from data collected monthly on vegetation and wildlife for over seven years (1972-1979) in order to design wildlife enhancement projects. Implementation of projects was conducted between 1979-1981 to gain information on costs, develop methodologies on revegetation, and to test model-generated predictions.

Anderson, M.T. 1985. Riparian management of coastal Pacific ecosystems. Pages 364-368 in Riparian Ecosystems and Their Management: Reconciling Conflicting Uses. Proceedings of the Symposium. US Dep. Agric., For. Serv. Gen. Tech. Rep. RM-120, 523pp. Rocky Mountain Forest and Range Experiment Station, Fort Collins, CO.

LOCATION: OR

KEYWORDS: COASTAL ECOSYSTEMS, FOREST

ABSTRACT

The Siskiyou National Forest in Oregon manages riparian areas along the Pacific coast where high value conifers stand near streams bearing salmonid fisheries. Riparian areas are managed by setting objectives which allows for limited timber harvest along with stream protection. The annual timber sale quantity from the Forest is reduced by 13 percent to protect riparian areas and the fishery resource.

Apple, L.L. 1985. Riparian habitat restoration and beavers. Pages 489-490 in Riparian Ecosystems and Their Management: Reconciling Conflicting Uses. Proceedings of the Symposium. US Dep. Agric. For. Serv. Gen. Tech. Rep. RM-120, 523pp. Rocky Mountain Forest and Range Experiment Station, Fort Collins, CO.

LOCATION: WY

KEYWORDS: BEAVER, HABITAT RESTORATION

ABSTRACT

This study was partially designed to determine whether materials could be supplied to beavers in marginal habitats, with resulting habitat improvement. The study was expanded to determine if both beavers and materials could be successfully relocated to these areas. The results have been very promising as a means of stabilizing and improving degraded riparian habitats.

Armour, C.L. 1977. Effects of deteriorated range streams on trout. US Dep. Inter., Bur. Land Manage. Idaho State Office, Boise, Idaho. 7pp.

LOCATION: ID

KEYWORDS: GRAZING IMPACTS

ABSTRACT

Improper management of domestic livestock on western ranges has caused habitat degradation of trout streams in some areas. As a result, there is either less trout production or conditions have deteriorated to such a degree that the fish can not survive in the streams. To accommodate requirements of sportsmen for additional fishing opportunities and to achieve national objectives for better balance in managing resources, it is necessary for habitat degradation problems to be solved.

Avery, E.L. 1983. A bibliography of beaver, trout, wildlife, and forest relationships: With special references to beaver and trout. Tech. Bull. 137, Department of Natural Resources, P.O. Box 7921, Madison, WI 53707. 23pp.

LOCATION: U.S. and CANADA

KEYWORDS: BEAVER-TROUT RELATIONSHIPS, WATERFOWL, WILDLIFE, FORESTS

ABSTRACT

A total of 446 references to beaver (Castor canadensis) ecology and the relationships of beaver to trout, waterfowl and other wildlife, and forests are presented. Annotations of 36 papers selected from the general references deal specifically with the relationship of beaver and their activities to wild trout in low to moderately high gradient streams in Wisconsin (10), Michigan (9), Minnesota (10), New York (5), Maine (2), Massachusetts (1), and Ontario (1).

Bayha, K.D. 1985. Riparian ecosystems of Alaska. Pages 491-492 <u>in</u> Riparian Ecosystems and Their Management: Reconciling Conflicting Uses. Proceedings of the Symposium. US Dep. Agric. For. Serv. Gen. Tech. Rep. RM-120, 523pp. Rocky Mountain Forest and Range Experiment Station, Fort Collins, CO.

LOCATION: AK

KEYWORDS: <u>ALASKA RIPARIAN ECOSYSTEMS</u>

ABSTRACT

The wide array of climatic conditions found in the Nation's largest state is illustrated by the equally wide variety of riparian ecosystems. As elsewhere, Alaska's riparian habitat are vital to a large variety of fish and wildlife species. Economic exploitation of natural resources also threatens Alaska's riparian ecosystems.

Behnke, R.J., and M. Zarn. 1976. Biology and Management of threatened and endangered western trouts. US Dep. Agric. For. Serv. Gen. Tech. Rep. RM-28, Rocky Mountain Forest and Range Experiment Station, Fort Collins, CO. 45pp.

LOCATION: WEST, U.S.

KEYWORDS: <u>NATIVE TROUT</u>

ABSTRACT

Discusses taxonomy, reasons for decline, life history and ecology, and suggestions for preservation and management of six closely related trouts native to western North America: Colorado River cutthroat, <u>Salmo clarki pleuriticus</u>; greenback trout, <u>S. c. stomias</u>; Lahontan cutthroat, <u>S. c. henshawi</u>; Paiute trout, <u>S. c. seleniris</u>; Gila trout, <u>S. gilae</u>; and Arizona native trout, <u>S. apache</u>. Meristic characters, distribution and status, habitat requirements and limiting factors, protective measures, and management recommendations are presented for each taxon.

Brehens-Tepper, J.C., J.T. O'Leary, and D.C. Andersen. 1985. Focused recreation use in riparian ecosystems: A taxonomy of user types. Pages 216-218. in Riparian Ecosystems and Their Management: Reconciling Conflicting Uses. Proceedings of the Symposium. US Dep. Agric. For. Serv. Gen. Tech. Rep. RM-120, 523pp. Rocky Mountain Forest and Range Experiment Station, Fort Collins, CO.

LOCATION: IN

KEYWORDS: RECREATION

ABSTRACT

Using data from the 1980 National Survey of Fishing, Hunting, and Wildlife Associated Recreation, this paper examines Indiana anglers by amount of participation at rivers and streams, sociodemographic background and conservation activity involvement. Each of these factors appears to facilitate identification of different user types that should be considered in managing and planning riparian environments.

Bock, J.H., and C.E. Bock. 1985. Patterns of reproduction in Wright's Sycamore. Pages 493-494 in Riparian Ecosystems and Their Management: Reconciling Conflicting Uses. Proceedings of the Symposium. US Dep. Agric. For. Serv. Gen. Tech. Rep. RM-120, 523pp. Rocky Mountain Forest and Range Experiment Station, Fort Collins, CO.

LOCATION: AZ

KEYWORDS: SYCAMORE, WRIGHT'S

ABSTRACT

In southeastern Arizona this tree produces large numbers of viable seeds that fall in a compact fruit shadow around parent individuals. Sexual reproduction usually fails due to drought or flash-flooding. Large numbers of seedlings and saplings grew in one site with permanent water and little flooding. Young trees grew in clumps, usually of similar-sized individuals, and away from mature tree canopy but always in the stream channel.

Brady, W., D.R. Patton, and J. Paxson. 1985. The development of southwestern riparian gallery forests. Pages 39-43. in Riparian Ecosystems and Their Management: Reconciling Conflicting Uses. Proceedings of the Symposium. US Dep. Agric. For. Serv. Gen. Tech. Rep. RM-120, 523pp. Rocky Mountain Forest and Range Experiment Station, Fort Collins, CO.

LOCATION: SOUTHWESTERN U.S.

KEYWORDS: RIPARIAN GALLERY FORESTS, OVERFLOW CHANNELS, FLOODING, AGGRADATION

ABSTRACT

Riparian gallery forests along two rivers in the southwestern United States are described in a developmental continum ranging from nursery bar to mature forest. Habitats suitable for tree reproduction are recognizable by their position relative to the active water course. These sites are typically located in overflow channels and receive flow only during floods. Flooding and the subsequent aggradation appear to be the major variables for the natural sequence of development within riparian stands.

Brook, J.H. 1985. Physical characteristics and pedogenesis of soils in riparian habitats along the upper Gila River Basin. Pages 49-53 in Riparian Ecosystems and Their Management: Reconciling Conflicting Uses. Proceedings of the Symposium. US Dep. Agric. For. Serv. Gen. Tech. Rep. RM-120, 523pp. Rocky Mountain Forest and Range Experiment Station, Fort Collins, CO.

LOCATION: AZ

KEYWORDS: SOIL, PHYSICAL CHARACTERISTICS

ABSTRACT

Knowledge of soils in southwest riparian habitats is minimal. Soil profiles in the riparian zone on the Gila and San Francisco Rivers were studied. The soils that support trees can be classified as Torrifluvents or on the more stable sites as Haplustolls. Coarse textures and low water holding capacity are dominant characteristics.

Brunsfeld, S.J., and F.D. Johnson. 1985. Field guide to the willows of east-central Idaho. University of Idaho, Bull. 39, College of Forestry, Wildlife and Range Sciences. Moscow, Idaho 83843 95pp.

LOCATION: ID

KEYWORDS: WILLOW, WILLOW FIELD GUIDE

ABSTRACT

This guide describes the willows of the upper Salmon River drainage in east-central Idaho. This area of about 8,000 square miles extends from the headwaters of the Salmon River to the mouth of the Middle Fork, including the Yankee Fork, East Fork, Pahsimeroi River, Lemhi River, North Fork, Panther Creek and numerous smaller tributaries. Two isolated streams that are part of the Snake River watershed, Birch Creek and the Little Lost River, are included in the southeastern corner of the study area.

Bryant, L.D. 1985. Livestock management in the riparian ecosystem. Pages 285-289. in Riparian Ecosystems and Their Management: Reconciling Conflicting Uses. Proceedings of the Symposium. US Dep. Agric. For. Serv. Gen. Tech. Rep. RM-120, 523pp. Rocky Mountain Forest and Range Experiment Station, Fort Collins, CO.

LOCATION: OR

KEYWORDS; PRODUCTION, GRAZING SYSTEMS

ABSTRACT

Intensive, long-term livestock grazing has occurred along most streams in the western United States. Although most livestock grazing on public lands is now under some form of management, many riparian areas are below "good" in ecologic condition, with forage production considerably below potential. Eight years of research at Meadow Creek, Starkey Experimental Forest and Range, Wallowa-Whitman National Forest, in northeastern Oregon, indicates that herbage production was increased 1- to 4-fold through timing and intensity of grazing. Rest-rotation, deferred rotation, and season-long grazing systems were tested. Although there were no statistically different changes in plant composition, the production of both graminoids and forbs increased dramatically.

Bryant, M.D. 1985. Changes 30 years after logging in large woody debris, and its use by salmonids. Pages 329-334 in Riparian Ecosystems and Their Management: Reconciling Conflicting Uses. Proceedings of the Symposium. US Dep. Agric. For. Serv. Gen. Tech. Rep. RM-120, 523pp. Rocky Mountain Forest and Range Experiment Station, Fort Collins, CO.

LOCATION: AK, BC

KEYWORDS: WOODY DEBRIS, LOGGING STUDY, STREAM SALMONID, LOGGING IMPACT

ABSTRACT

Changes in large woody debris in fourth and fifth-order salmon streams with logged, unlogged, and partially logged riparian zones are documented from maps--for 1949 and 1960--and from field surveys done in 1983 and 1984. Over the 30-year period, most changes in the amount of large woody debris in the logged systems. During and immediately after logging large increases were noted, but in 1984 the amount of large woody debris in the logged systems was less than that observed before logging in most categories. Amounts of large woody debris in the other streams remained relatively stable. Thirty years after logging, habitat formed as a result of large debris provides important rearing areas for juvenile salmonids. Results from this study emphasize the importance of managing riparian zones as a source of large organic debris.

Buckhouse, J.C. 1985. Water and people: Common denominators in riparian zones. Pages 369-370 in Riparian Ecosystems and Their Management: Reconciling Conflicting Uses. Proceedings of the Symposium. US Dep. Agric. For. Serv. Gen. Tech. Rep. RM-120, 523pp. Rocky Mountain Forest and Range Experiment Station, Fort Collins, CO.

LOCATION: OR

KEYWORDS: PLANNING

ABSTRACT

Water can be allocated according to any number of approaches. People are harder to manage since they work from diverse social, psychological, economic, and aesthetic backgrounds. An approach which brings people together makes the most sense for multiple use management.

Christensen, K.M. 1985. The linear interval method for determining habitat selection of riparian wildlife species. Pages 101-104 in Riparian Ecosystems and Their Management: Reconciling Conflicting Uses. Proceedings of the Symposium. US Dep. Agric. For. Serv. Gen. Tech. Rep. RM-120, 523pp. Rocky Mountain Forest and Range Experiment Station, Fort Collins, CO.

LOCATION: AZ

KEYWORDS: LINEAR INTERVAL, WILDLIFE, RIPARIAN HABITAT

ABSTRACT

Since this technique (originally developed for river otters) can be used in highly hetergeneous habitats, incorporates both categorical and continuous data, yields a physiognomic representation of habitat structure, and facilitates the use of multivariate statistics in data analysis, it is inherently superior to those techniques typically employed by wildlife ecologies in studies of habitat selection.

Cope, O.B. 1979. Grazing and riparian/stream ecosystems-A forum. Trout Unlimited Inc., Denver, Co. 94pp.

LOCATION: WESTERN U.S.

KEYWORDS: GRAZING IMPACTS, PUBLIC USERS, MANAGEMENT TECHNIQUES, RIPARIAN EXCLOSURES, FEDERAL LAND MANAGEMENT POLICY

ABSTRACT

21 papers, 94 pages discussing the impacts of livestock grazing on riparian areas and the solutions to the problem.

Cowardin, L.M., V. Carter, F.C. Golet, and E.T. LaRoe. 1979.
Classification of wetlands and deepwater habitats of the United
States. Office of Biological Services, Fish and Wildl. Serv., U.S.
Dep. Inter., Washington, DC. 20240. 103pp.

LOCATION: U.S.

KEYWORDS: WETLANDS CLASSIFICATION, DEEPWATER HABITATS, HYDROPHYTES,
HYDRIC SOILS

AUTHOR ABBREVIATED ABSTRACT

This classification, to be used in a new inventory of wetlands
and deepwater habitats of the United States, is intended to describe
ecological taxa, arrange them in a system useful to resource
managers, furnish units for mapping, and provide uniformity of
concepts and terms. Wetlands are defined by plants (hydrophytes),
soils (hydric soils), and frequency of flooding. Ecologically
related areas of deep water, traditionally not considered wetlands,
are included in the classification as deepwater habitats.

Cox, J.R., and H.L. Morton. 1985. Above-ground biomass quantities and
livestock production at big sacaton riparian areas in southeastern
Arizona. Pages 305-309 in Riparian Ecosystems and Their
Management: Reconciling Conflicting Uses. Proceedings of the
Symposium. US Dep. Agric. For. Serv. Gen. Tech. Rep. RM-120, 523pp.
Rocky Mountain Forest and Range Experiment Station, Fort Collins, CO.

LOCATION: AZ

KEYWORDS: GRAZING, BIG SACATON BIOMASS

ABSTRACT

Two big sacaton (Sporobolus wrightii) grassland riparian sites
were studied in southeastern Arizona. At site I we measured green
biomass, dead standing and standing crops of big sacaton for 3
years. At site II we annually burned or mowed big sacaton pastures
in February and annually grazed these pastures plus an untreated
control pasture between 1 May and 15 July for three years. Green
biomass peaked in August at 1300 and 3000 kg/ha in dry and wet years,
respectively. Dead standing biomass accumulated in the fall and
disappeared following either fall, winter or summer precipitation.
Standing crop (green plus dead standing) was greatest in August and
averaged 4400 kg/ha. Both burning and mowing reduced green biomass
production. Stocking rates on burned and mowed pastures were only
one-third as high as on untreated. Mean daily gains in 1981 and 1982
averaged 0.41 and 0.67 kg/day on untreated and treated pastures,
respectively, but total gains per pasture were 512 and 235 kg on the
untreated and treated, respectively.

Cross, S.P. 1985. Responses of small mammals to forest riparian perturbations. Pages 269-275 in Riparian Ecosystems and Their Management: Reconciling Conflicting Uses. Proceedings of the Symposium. US Dep. Agric. For. Serv. Gen. Tech. Rep. RM-120, 523 p. Rocky Mountain Forest and Range Experiment Station, Fort Collins, CO.

LOCATION: OR

KEYWORDS: PERTURBATIONS, MAMMALS SMALL, FOREST

ABSTRACT

Trapping studies at several mixed conifer forest sites in southwestern Oregon demonstrate a differentially high use of riparian habitat by small mammals. Harsh perturbations of this habitat radically affect the presence and abundance of many species. Riparian leave-strips were found to support small-mammal communities comparable to undisturbed sites.

Crouse, M.R., and R.R. Kindschy. 1981. A method for predicting riparian vegetation potential of semiarid rangelands. Pages 110-116 in Acquisition and Utilization of Aquatic Habitat Inventory Information. Proceedings of a Symposium, October 28-30, 1981, Western Div. of Am. Fish Soc. Portland, OR 375pp.

LOCATION: OR

KEYWORDS: POTENTIAL VEGETATION

ABSTRACT

Predicting the potential of riparian areas to recover after protection from livestock is difficult because examples of pristine riparian communities have generally been destroyed by excessive grazing. This paper describes a method for predicting riparian site potential of streams and reservoirs in semiarid climates such as southeastern Oregon. The method is based on physical characteristics of stream and reservoir riparian zones, such as extent of water level fluctuation, persistence of flow, scouring, and soil type. These factors have been organized into keys for field use. Predicting the potential of riparian sites is essential to set priorities for the expenditure of funds to enhance and monitor those sites.

Cuplin, P. 1981. The use of large scale color infrared photography for stream habitat and riparian vegetation inventory. Tech. Note 325, US Dep. Inter., Bur. Land Manage., Bldg. 50, Denver Federal Center, Denver, CO., 80225, 7pp.

LOCATION: U.S.

KEYWORDS: STREAM HABITAT, INVENTORY, PHOTOGRAPHY INFRARED COLOR

ABSTRACT

A system of ground data sampling and photointerpretation of stream habitat and riparian vegetation is described. Ground data samples are the basis for photointerpretation and classification of stream habitat and riparian vegetation. Stream habitat is classified for each stream mile by condition class of poor, fair, good, or excellent. Riparian vegetation is classified by dominant and sub-dominant plant species, delineated, and number of acres calculated by using a dot grid or planimeter.

Cuplin, P. 1985. Riparian area inventory and monitoring using large scale color infrared photography. Pages 69-71 in Riparian Ecosystems and Their Management: Reconciling Conflicting Uses. Proceedings of the Symposium. US Dep. Agric. For. Serv. Gen. Tech. Rep. RM-120, 523pp. Rocky Mountain Forest and Range Experiment Station, Fort Collins, CO.

LOCATION: WESTERN U.S.

KEYWORDS: REMOTE SENSING, INVENTORY, MONITORING, AIRPHOTOS, PHOTOGRAPHY COLOR INFRARED

ABSTRACT

Variables that can be photointerpreted from large scale color infrared airphotos with ground data and used to monitor change in stream/riparian areas are stream width; floodplain width; stream channel stability; stream bank stability; stream shade; ground cover of trees, shrubs, and herbaceous vegetation; bare soil; riparian area and width; and density and structure of large trees and shrubs.

Cuplin, P., W.S. Platts, O. Casey, and R. Masinton. 1985. A comparison of riparian area ground data with large scale airphoto interpretation. Pages 67-68 in Riparian Ecosystems and Their Management: Reconciling Conflicting Uses. Proceedings of the Symposium. US Dep. Agric. For. Serv. Gen. Tech. Rep. RM-120, 523pp. Rocky Mountain Forest and Range Experiment Station, Fort Collins, CO.

LOCATION: NV

KEYWORDS: REMOTE SENSING, AIRPHOTOS SCALE LARGE, AIRPHOTO INTERPRETATION

ABSTRACT

A study site on Tabor Creek in northeast Nevada has been monitored by ground data collection each year since 1979. Airphotos of the study site were acquired in large scale (1:2,000 color) infrared 9- x 9-inch format during July 1984. Ground data and airphoto interpretation are compared.

Dahlem, E.A. 1979. The Mahogany Creek watershed--With and without grazing. Pages 31-34 in O.B. Cope. ed. Grazing and Riparian/ Stream Ecosystems: Proceedings of the Forum. Trout Unlimited Inc., Denver, CO. 94pp.

LOCATION: NV

KEYWORDS: LIVESTOCK GRAZING, LIVESTOCK EXCLUSION, HABITAT IMPROVEMENT

REVIEWER'S ABSTRACT

The attraction that riparian areas have for domestic livestock has long been noted by wildlife biologists and livestock managers. The high moisture content of riparian vegetation makes it extremely palatable to livestock, especially in summer when surrounding rangelands are desiccated. The tendency for livestock, especially cattle, to congregate along riparian areas is reinforced by the fact that, in mountainous areas, streams are often located in narrow canyons with steep slopes on both sides. These factors invariably lead to overgrazing and abuse of riparian areas. Such as the case along Mahogany Creek and its watershed, located in northwest Humbolt County, Nevada. The reduction in livestock grazing, but continued annual use, had little beneficial effect on riparian habitat along Mahogany Creek. Only after complete removal of livestock use by fencing was significant riparian habitat improvement accomplished along Mahogany Creek.

DeBano, L.F., J.J. Brejda, and J.H. Brock. 1984. Enhancement of riparian vegetation following shrub control in Arizona chaparral. in J. of Soil and Water Cons. 39(5)317-320.

LOCATION: AZ

KEYWORDS: CHAPARRAL, SHRUB CONTROL

ABSTRACT

The effect of upstream shrub control on the establishment of riparian vegetation was evaluated on a chaparral watershed in central Arizona. After 20 years of increased streamflow and longer duration streamflow, a riparian zone below the watershed treated for shrub control had 7 riparian plants per 100 m^2 compared with the nearby, untreated watershed that had 2.3 plants per 100 m^2. The increase in riparian vegetation has implications for water quality, wildlife, and water use.

DeByle, N.V., and R.P. Winokur, editors. 1985. Aspen: Ecology and management in the western United States. US For. Serv. Gen. Tech. Rep. RM-119, 283pp. Rocky Mountain Forest and Range Experiment Station, Fort Collins, CO.

LOCATION: U.S. and CANADA

KEYWORDS: ASPEN, ASPEN FOREST TYPE

ABSTRACT

Information about the biology, ecology, and management of quaking aspen on the mountains and plateaus of the interior western United States, and to a lesser extent, Canada is summarized and discussed. The biology of aspen as a tree species, community relationships in the aspen ecosystem, environments, and factors affecting aspen forests are reviewed. The resources available within and from the aspen forest type, and their past and potential uses are examined. Silvicultural methods and other approaches to managing aspen for various resources and uses are presented.

Dickson, J.G., and J.C. Huntley. 1985. Streamside management zones and wildlife in the southern coastal plain. Pages 263-264 in Riparian Ecosystems and Their Management: Reconciling Conflicting Uses. Proceedings of the Symposium. US Dep. Agric. For. Serv. Gen. Tech. Rep. RM-120, 523pp. Rocky Mountain Forest and Range Experiment Station, Fort Collins, CO.

LOCATION: TX

KEYWORDS: STREAMSIDE MANAGEMENT, VEGETATION COMPOSITION

ABSTRACT

We are assessing the impacts of presence and vegetative composition of Streamside Management Zones (SMZ) on squirrels, deer, furbearers, small mammals, birds, reptiles, and amphibians. Preliminary results for squirrels show gray and fox squirrels were abundant in the wide SMZ, but virtually absent from medium and narrow SMZ.

Dileanis, P.D., F.A. Branson, and S.K. Sorenson. 1985. Methods for determining effects of controlled dewatering of shallow aquifers on desert phreatophytes on Owens Valley, California. Pages 197-200 in Riparian Ecosystems and Their Management: Reconciling Conflicting Uses. Proceedings of the Symposium. US Dep. Agric. For. Serv. Gen. Tech. Rep. RM-120, 523pp. Rocky Mountain Forest and Range Experiment Station, Fort Collins, CO.

LOCATION: CA

KEYWORDS: PHREATOPHYTES, DEWATERING

ABSTRACT

The ability of phreatophytic plants to tolerate and survive dewatering of shallow aquifers is being tested. At test sites that have been equipped with pumping wells, soil moisture and plant physiological responses are being measured as water levels decline.

Disano, J., B.W. Anderson, J.K. Meents, and R.D. Ohmart. 1984. Compatibility of biofuel production with wildlife habitat enhancement. Pages 739-743 in California Riparian Systems: Ecology, Conservation, and Productive Management. Warner, R.E. and K. Hendrix, eds. University of California Press. Berkeley, CA. 1035pp.

LOCATION: CA

KEYWORDS: WILDLIFE HABITAT ENHANCEMENT, BIOFUEL PRODUCTION

ABSTRACT

A stand of native cottonwood trees (Populus fremontii) with hedges of quail bush (Atriplex lentiformis) would attract high avian densities and diversities. Densities and diversities of birds and rodents reached above-average levels for riparian vegetation in the lower Colorado River valley within two years from planting on two experimental plots and within one year on a third plot. The rapid growth rate of native trees and the acceptance of revegetated areas by wildlife, in conjunction with the current demand for wood as fuel, suggests that the two objectives are compatible and the latter can be economically productive.

Dobson, A.T. 1973. Changes in the structure of a riparian community as the result of grazing. Pages 58-64 in Proceedings of the New Zealand Ecological Society. Vol. 20

LOCATION: NEW ZEALAND

KEYWORDS: GRAZING IMPACT, RIPARIAN COMMUNITY STRUCTURE

ABSTRACT

This describes changes due to grazing that occurred in the vegetation and topography of a previously ungrazed, riparian site. Grazing made the site more susceptible to erosion by eliminating the main pioneer species. Phalaris arundinacea, a rhizomatous reed grass.

Duell, L.F., Jr., and D.M. Nork. 1985. Comparison of three micro-
meteorological methods to calculate evapotranspiration in Owens
Valley California. Pages 161-165 in Riparian Ecosystems and Their
Management: Reconciling Conflicting Uses. Proceedings of the
Symposium. US Dep. Agric. For. Serv. Gen. Tech. Rep. RM-120, 523pp.
Rocky Mountain Forest and Range Experiment Station, Fort Collins, CO.

LOCATION: CA

KEYWORDS: EVAPOTRANSPIRATION, OWENS VALLEY, MICROMETEORLOGICAL

ABSTRACT

Using the Bowen ratio/energy-budget, eddy-correlation, and Penman
combination methods, 24-hour evapotranspiration values, in
millimeters per day, were 6.1, 6.0, and 21.7 for a salt grass site in
May 1984; 1.2, 2.0, and 12.3 for a greasewood site in June 1984; and
1.6, 2.2, and 10.4 for a rabbitbrush site in July 1984.

Duff, D.A., and J.L. Cooper. 1976. Techniques for conducting stream
habitat surveys on National Resource Land. US Dep. Inter., Bur. Land
Manage. Tech. Note 283, Bldg. 50, Federal Center, Denver, CO 80225.
73pp.

LOCATION: U.S.

KEYWORDS: STREAM SURVEY

ABSTRACT

This technical note provides guidance and standards for
conducting certain types of aquatic habitat surveys on national
resource lands administered by the Bureau of Land Management. The
objectives are to provide adequate procedures designed to evaluate
most of the common environmental conditions that limit aquatic
habitat and fish production and to assure that aquatic habitat
resources, including water quality, is given adequate consideration
in the management of resources on national resource lands.

Duff, D.A. 1979. Riparian habitat recovery on Big Creek, Rich County, Utah—A summary of 8 years of study. Pages 91-92 in Cope, O.B. ed. Grazing and Riparian/Stream Ecosystems: Proceedings of the Forum. Trout Unlimited Inc., Denver, CO. 94pp.

LOCATION: UT

KEYWORDS: STREAM EXCLOSURE, LIVESTOCK GRAZING, GRAZING IMPACTS

ABSTRACT

In 1970 the Bureau of Land Management constructed a 0.4-km (0.25 mi) riparian zone exclosure, fencing off 1,006 meters (3,300 ft) of stream channel from livestock use on Big Creek, Rich County, Utah, to monitor the recovery of riparian habitat from livestock-grazing impacts. Seventeen stream improvement structures were placed in the stream inside the exclosure in 1970 and an additional 26 structures were placed inside and outside the exclosure in 1971 to help accelerate recovery of badly eroded streambank soil conditions, as well as improve pool quality for resident fisheries. Habitat studies from 1973 to 1978 have shown the habitat inside the exclosure to recover significantly from rest, while areas outside the exclosure continue to decline as a result of continued livestock use.

Elder, R.G., and R.C. Moore. 1985. Impacts of oil and gas development on riparian zones in the overthrust belt: The role of industrial siting. Pages 379-383 in Riparian Ecosystems and Their Management: Reconciling Conflicting Uses. Proceedings of the Symposium. US Dep. Agric. For. Serv. Gen. Tech. Rep. RM-120, 523pp. Rocky Mountain Forest and Range Experiment Station, Fort Collins, CO.

LOCATION: WY

KEYWORDS: OIL AND GAS DEVELOPMENT, OVERTHRUST BELT, INDUSTRIAL SITING

ABSTRACT

As oil and gas development in the Overthrust Belt of Wyoming expands, the need to minimize impacts to riparian systems becomes increasingly important. However, regulatory control is sometimes ineffectual. Because of its broad powers, the Industrial Siting process can play a key role in mitigating environmental impacts that are otherwise unregulated.

England, A.S., L.D. Foreman, and W.F. Laudenslayer, Jr. 1984. Composition and abundance of bird populations in riparian systems of the California deserts. Pages 694-705 in Warner, R.E. and K.M. Hendrix eds. California Riparian Systems: Ecology, Conservation, and Productive Management. University of California Press, Berkeley, CA.

LOCATION: CA

KEYWORDS: BIRD POPULATIONS, DESERTS

ABSTRACT

Avian population diversity, density, and species richness in desert riparian systems were analyzed using 73 breeding bird surveys, 62 winter bird-population studies, and biweekly surveys at 15 sites. Breeding bird surveys indicated that cottonwood/willow vegetation-types had the highest number of breeding and visiting species and the highest bird diversity among desert vegetation-types. Willow had the highest bird density. Winter bird-population studies showed that cottonwood/willow also had the species richness and diversity during winter, but palm and palo verde/ironwood had higher bird densities. All population variables were higher in desert riparian systems than in non-riparian desert vegetation-types during winter and breeding seasons.

Fenner, P., W.W. Brady, and D.R. Patton. 1984. Observations on seeds and seedlings of Fremont Cottonwood. Desert Plants 6(1):55-58.

LOCATION: AZ

KEYWORDS: COTTONWOOD, SEED GERMINATION

ABSTRACT

The seeds of Fremont Cottonwood (Populus fremontii) lose viability within 1 to 5 weeks after dispersal. Moisture stress induced by osmotic solutions stronger than six atmospheres both delayed and reduced total germination. Root growth rates of young seedlings averaged 6 mm per day. Because of the limited time of seed viability, a suitable substrate for germination must occur at or soon after seed dispersal. Moist conditions must persist until seedling roots grow to depths where moisture is more constantly available than near the surface.

Fenner, P., W.W. Brady, and D.R. Patton. 1985. Effects of regulated water flows on regeneration of Fremont Cottonwood. J. of Range Manage. 38(2):135-138.

LOCATION: AZ

KEYWORDS: COTTONWOOD FREMONT, REGULATED WATER FLOWS, COTTONWOOD REGENERATION

ABSTRACT

The reduction in extent of riparian forests in the southwestern United States has been a topic of recent concern. The effect of dams on downstream river flow and the consequent modification of the riparian habitat was studied along the lower Salt River in central Arizona. Dams were found to change the magnitude of river flows and change the seasonal timing of flows in such a way that the habitat appeared less adapted for regeneration of Populus fremontii. Modification of river flow pattern, therefore, appears likely to have been a significant factor causing change in vegetation along Salt River.

Field, D.R., M.E. Lee, and K. Martinson. 1985. Human behavior and recreation habitats: Conceptual issues. Pages 227-231 in Riparian Ecosystems and Their Management: Reconciling Conflicting Uses. Proceedings of the Symposium. US Dep. Agric. For. Serv. Gen. Tech. Rep. RM-120, 523pp. Rocky Mountain Forest and Range Experiment Station, Fort Collins, CO.

LOCATION: CA

KEYWORDS: RECREATION

ABSTRACT

Individual recreation behavior and recreation experiences are more often than not determined by three sets of factors: the social group within which an individual participates, including the mix of social groups occupying a specific recreation place; the biological or physical characteristics of that place; and the management prescriptions applied there. Few studies have examined recreation behavior in the context of these three sets of factors. The present paper provides a conceptual framework to do so. The focus is upon human behavior and recreation habitats. Human ecological principles, along with concepts used to classify recreation "habitats" according to the recreation opportunities they provide, form the conceptual framework for the presentation.

Finch, D.M. 1985. A weighted-means ordination of riparian birds in Southeastern Wyoming. Pages 495-498 in Riparian Ecosystems and Their Management: Reconciling Conflicting Uses. Proceedings of the Symposium. US Dep. Agric. For. Serv. Gen. Tech. Rep. RM-120, 523pp. Rocky Mountain Forest and Range Experiment Station, Fort Collins, CO.

LOCATION: WY

KEYWORDS: RIPARIAN BIRDS, BIRD DISTRIBUTION

ABSTRACT

Variation among habitat associations of 31 riparian bird species in southeastern Wyoming was analyzed using a weighted-means ordination. Three principal components explained 86.7% of the variation among habitat associations of bird species. The components showed high positive loadings for variables associated with canopy, shrub size, and vegetation height.

Garcia, J.C. 1985. A method for assessing the value of stream corridors to fish and wildlife resources. Pages 335-338 in Riparian Ecosystems and Their Management: Reconciling Conflicting Uses. Proceedings of the Symposium. US Dep. Agric. For. Serv. Gen. Tech. Rep. RM-120, 523pp. Rocky Mountain Forest and Range Experiment Station, Fort Collins, CO.

LOCATION: CA

KEYWORDS: STREAM CORRIDOR EVALUATION

ABSTRACT

SCIES provides a method for fish and wildlife managers to measure the habitat value of stream corridors, quantifying in explicit terms many complex values and factors. It was developed to have broad applications, to be flexible, to be capable of incorporating existing methods and knowledge, and to be comprehensive, easy to use, and verifiable.

Gibbons, D.R., and E.O. Salo. 1973. An annotated bibliography of the effects of logging on fish of the Western United States and Canada. US For. Serv. Gen. Tech. Rep. PNW-10, Pacific Northwest Forest and Range Experiment Station, Portland, OR. 145pp.

LOCATION: WESTERN U.S.

KEYWORDS: STREAMSIDE VEGETATION, STREAM PROTECTION, STREAM IMPROVEMENT, LOGGING IMPACTS, MULTIPLE USE

ABSTRACT

This bibliography is an annotation of the scientific and nonscientific literature published on the effects of logging on fish and aquatic habitat of the Western United States and Canada. It includes 278 annotations and 317 total references. Subject areas include erosion and sedimentation, water quality, related influences upon salmonids, multiple logging effects, alteration of streamflow, stream protection, multiple-use management, streamside vegetation, stream improvement, and descriptions of studies on effects of logging. A review of the literature, a narrative on the state of the art, and a list of research needs determined by questionnaires are included.

Gibbons, D.R. 1985. The fish habitat management unit concept for streams on National Forests in Alaska. Pages 320-323 in Riparian Ecosystems and Their Management: Reconciling Conflicting Uses. Proceedings of the Symposium. US Dep. Agric. For. Serv. Gen. Tech. Rep. RM-120, 523pp. Rocky Mountain Forest and Range Experiment Station, Fort Collins, CO.

LOCATION: AK

KEYWORDS: FISH HABITAT MANAGEMENT UNIT, FOREST

ABSTRACT

The occurrence of alternatives invariably exists between the management of timber and fisheries resources. The concept of Fish Habitat Management Units (FHMU's) has been developed on National Forest Lands in Alaska to describe the specific streamside management requirements needed for the maintenance and improvement of aquatic resources. This paper discusses the development and management applications of FHMU's.

Gillen, R.L., W.C. Krueger, and R.F. Miller. 1985. Cattle use of riparian meadows in the Blue Mountains of northeastern Oregon. J. of Range Manage. 38(3):205-209.

LOCATION: OR

KEYWORDS: RIPARIAN MEADOWS, GRAZING IMPACT, SEASON OF USE, GRAZING

AUTHOR/ABBREVIATED ABSTRACT

The intensity and pattern of cattle use of small riparian meadows were studied by periodically sampling vegetative standing crop and by continuously monitoring meadows with time-lapse photography. Temperature and relative humidity were also measured in riparian and upland plant communities. Herbage standing crop at the end of the grazing season was similar under continuous grazing and the early and late grazing periods of a two pasture deferred rotation grazing system. Early grazing tended to decrease the total cattle occupation and the frequency of cattle occupation of riparian meadows when compared to continuous grazing.

Groeneveld, D.P., and T.E. Griepentrog. 1985. Interdependence of ground-water, riparian vegetation and streambank stability: A case study. Pages 44-48 in Riparian Ecosystems and Their Management: Reconciling Conflicting Uses. Proceedings of the Symposium. US Dep. Agric. For. Serv. Gen. Tech. Rep. RM-120, 523pp. Rocky Mountain Forest and Range Experiment Station, Fort Collins, CO.

LOCATION: CA

KEYWORDS: GROUNDWATER, VEGETATION, STREAMBANK STABILITY

ABSTRACT

Groundwater is closely coupled with streamflow to maintain water supply to riparian vegetation, particularly where precipitation is seasonal. A case study is presented where Mediterranean climate and groundwater extraction are linked with the decline of riparian vegetation and subsequent severe bank erosion on the Carmel River in Carmel Valley, California.

Groeneveld, D.P., D.L. Grate, P.J. Hubbard, D.S. Munk, P.J. Novak, B. Tillemans, D.C. Watten, and I. Yamashita. 1985. A field assessment of above- and below-ground factors affecting phreatophyte transpiration in the Owens Valley, California. Pages 166-170 in Riparian Ecosystems and Their Management: Reconciling Conflicting Uses. Proceedings of the Symposium. US Dep. Agric. For. Serv. Gen. Tech. Rep. RM-120, 523pp. Rocky Mountain Forest and Range Experiment Station, Fort Collins, CO.

LOCATION: CA

KEYWORDS: TRANSPIRATION, PHREATOPHYTES, GROUNDWATER, CANOPY FACTORS, ROOT DENSITY

ABSTRACT

Factors influencing the water balance physiology and transpiration of five Great Basin shrub and grass phreatophytes are being investigated in shallow groundwater zones of the arid Owens Valley, California. Measurements of transpiration, atmospheric potential, canopy factors, root density, soil moisture and xylem potential are presented and discussed.

Hair, J.D., G.T. Hepp, L.M. Luckett, K.P. Reese, and D.K. Woodward. 1978. Beaver pond ecosystems and their relationships to multi-use natural resource management. Pages 80-92 in Strategies for Protection and Management of Floodplain Wetlands and Other Riparian Ecosystems. Johnson, R.R. and J.R. McCormick, tech. coords. Proc. symp. Callaway Gardens, GA. US Dep. Agric., For. Serv. Gen. Tech. Rep. WO-12.

LOCATION: NC

KEYWORDS: BEAVER POND ECOSYSTEMS, MULTIPLE-USE, WETLAND HABITATS

ABSTRACT

Thousands of hectares of land have been impounded by beavers in the southeastern United States. Significant economic losses to agribusiness and forest production have been reported. However, beaver impoundments are valuable components of many regional riparian ecosystems and provide numerous opportunities for multi-use management programs. As a renewable fur resource, beaver populations should be regulated through an annual sustained harvest. Beaver impoundments are important wetland habitats and have higher avian diversity values than adjacent upland areas. They can be effectively managed for waterfowl hunting and with increased importance of non-consumptive utilization of wildlife resources, they provide numerous opportunities for development of natural resource education programs.

Harris, R.R., R.J. Risser, and C.A. Fox. 1985. A method for evaluating streamflow discharge--Plant species occurrence patterns on headwater streams. Pages 87-90 in Riparian Ecosystems and Their Management: Reconciling Conflicting Uses. Proceedings of the Symposium. US Dep. Agric. For. Serv. Gen. Tech. Rep. RM-120, 523pp. Rocky Mountain Forest and Range Experiment Station, Fort Collins, CO.

LOCATION: CA

KEYWORDS: HYDROELECTRIC PROJECTS, INSTREAM FLOW, STREAM DISCHARGE

ABSTRACT

On headwater streams proposed or developed for hydroelectric projects, hydrologic simulation modeling (Instream Flow Incremental Method) can be used in conjunction with vegetation sampling to assist in the evaluation of instream flow requirements for riparian plant species. Field studies on the western and eastern slopes of the Sierra Nevada have been undertaken to test the method and have shown promising results.

Harvey, D.M., C.C. Watson, and S.A. Schumm. 1985. Gully erosion. US Dep. Inter., Bur. Land Manage., Denver Service Center, Division of Resource Systems, Tech. Note 366, Denver, CO 80225.

LOCATION: WESTERN U.S.

KEYWORDS: GULLY EROSION

ABSTRACT

Many land uses, including livestock grazing and surface mining, may influence gully erosion processes. Land managers often require information on the stages of gully evolution, current stability of gully systems, and estimates of long-term gully erosion rates and sediment yields. While there are very few standardized methods for evaluating gully systems, a great deal of information on gully erosion processes has been generated. The purpose of this report is to make information on gully erosion available to resource specialists and provide a conceptual framework to help evaluate gully systems and gully erosion processes.

Heede, B.H. 1985. Interactions between streamside vegetation and stream dynamics. Pages 54-58 in Riparian Ecosystems and Their Management: Reconciling Conflicting Uses. Proceedings of the Symposium. US Dep. Agric. For. Serv. Gen. Tech. Rep. RM-120, 523pp. Rocky Mountain Forest and Range Experiment Station, Fort Collins, CO.

LOCATION: OR

KEYWORDS: HYDROLOGY, CHANNEL STABILITY, BEDLOAD, WATER QUALITY, LOGS IN STREAMS

ABSTRACT

Interrelationships between vegetation and hydrologic processes in riparian ecosystems must be considered by managers before they attempt to alter these natural systems. A 5-year experiment demonstrated that logs that fall across the channel from streamside forests dissipate flow energy, maintain channel stability, decrease bedload movement, and increase water quality.

Hoover, S.L., D.A. King, and W.J. Matter. 1985. A wilderness riparian environment: Visitor satisfaction, perceptions, reality, and management. Pages 223-226 in Riparian Ecosystems and Their Management: Reconciling Conflicting Uses. Proceedings of the Symposium. US Dep. Agric. For. Serv. Gen. Tech. Rep. RM-120, 523pp. Rocky Mountain Forest and Range Experiment Station, Fort Collins, CO.

LOCATION: AZ

KEYWORDS: WILDERNESS, RECREATION, VISITOR SATISFACTION

ABSTRACT

Visitors to the area were generally satisfied with their visits, but cited features associated with cattle, fishing and contact with other people as detractants. Their perceptions of the relative abundance of selected environmental conditions closely matched real-world measures. Attributes given the highest desirability ratings by the users were largely features likely to be prevalent in healthy riparian systems. Thus, management which maintains or enhances the ecological integrity of riparian areas may also contribute to their potential recreational values.

Horton, J.S., and C.J. Campbell. 1974. Management of phreatophyte and riparian vegetation for maximum multiple use values. US Dep. Agric. For. Serv. Res. Paper RM-117, Rocky Mountain Forest and Range Experiment Station, Fort Collins, CO. 23pp.

LOCATION: WESTERN U.S.

KEYWORDS: PHREATOPHYTES, VEGETATION, WATER YIELD IMPROVEMENT

ABSTRACT

Summarizes the status of our knowledge about environmental relations of vegetation along water courses in the southwestern United States, and impacts of vegetation management to reduce evapotranspiration on other resource values. Reviews the literature on measurement and evaluation of water losses from moist-site vegetation, ecological relationships, other resource uses of phreatophyte and riparian areas, and control methods. Suggests approaches to management of moist-site areas by zones based primarily on water table depth, elevation and tree species.

Hubert, W.A., R.P. Lanka, T.A. Wesche, and F. Stabler. 1985. Grazing management influences on two brook trout streams in Wyoming. Pages 290-294 in Riparian Ecosystems and Their Management: Reconciling Conflicting Uses. Proceedings of the Symposium. US Dep. Agric. For. Serv. Gen. Tech. Rep. RM-120, 523pp. Rocky Mountain Forest and Range Experiment Station, Fort Collins, CO.

LOCATION: WY

KEYWORDS: TROUT STREAM, GRAZING IMPACT

ABSTRACT

Brook trout abundance and instream habitat characteristics were evaluated in two rangeland streams. Heavily grazed and lightly grazed reaches of two streams with different grazing management were compared. Relationships between stream morphology, riparian zone characteristics, and trout abundance were observed.

Hunter, W.C., B.W. Anderson, and R.D. Ohmart. 1985. Summer avian community composition of tamarix habitats in three southwestern desert riparian systems. Pages 128-134 in Riparian Ecosystems and Their Management: Reconciling Conflicting Uses. Proceedings of the Symposium. US Dep. Agric. For. Serv. Gen. Tech. Rep. RM-120, 523pp. Rocky Mountain Forest and Range Experiment Station, Fort Collins, CO.

LOCATION: AZ, NV

KEYWORDS: TAMARIX, SALT CEDAR, AVIAN COMMUNITY, SOUTHWESTERN DESERT

ABSTRACT

Data from three southwestern river systems were used to assess avian response to salt cedar (Tamarix chinensis). Species were grouped by breeding biology and groups responded differently in their occurrence in salt cedar among the valleys. Biogeographical and climatic factors may explain these differences.

Jackson, W.L., and B.P. Van Haveren. 1985. Design for a stable channel in coarse alluvium for riparian zone restoration. Water Resour. Bull. 20(5):695-703.

LOCATION: CO

KEYWORDS: RESTORATION, HYDROLOGY, STREAM CHANNEL

AUTHOR/ABBREVIATED ABSTRACT

Geomorphic, hydraulic and hydrologic principles are applied in the design of a stable stream channel for a badly disturbed portion of Badger Creek, Colorado, and its associated riparian and meadow complexes. The objective is to shorten the period of time required for a channel in coarse alluvium to recover from an impacted morphologic state to a regime condition representative of current watershed conditions. Channel geometry measurements describe the stream channel and the normal bankfull stage in relatively stable reaches.

Jahn, L.R. 1978. Values of riparian habitats to natural ecosystems. Pages 157-160 in Strategies for Protection and Management of Floodplain Wetlands and Other Riparian Ecosystems. Johnson, R.R. and J.F. McCormick, tech. coords. Proc. symp. Callaway Gardens, GA. US Dep. Agric. For. Serv. Gen. Tech. Rep. WO-12. Washington DC. 410pp.

LOCATION: U.S.

KEYWORDS: NATURAL ECOSYSTEMS, VEGETATION, AQUATIC COMMUNITIES

ABSTRACT

Vegetation in riparian habitats stabilizes soils and supplies organic matter that sustains aquatic communities. Nutrient-rich silt deposited periodically is these habitats by floodwaters enriches soils that support bottomland hardwood forests, forage for wildlife and livestock, and outdoor recreation. Broader applications of management guidelines are required to adjust human-related activities in riparian zones.

Jakle, M.D., and T.A. Gatz. 1985. Herpetofaunal use of four habitats of the middle Gila River Drainage, Arizona. Pages 355-358 in Riparian Ecosystems and Their Management: Reconciling Conflicting Uses. Proceedings of the Symposium. US Dep. Agric. For. Serv. Gen. Tech. Rep. RM-120, 523pp. Rocky Mountain Forest and Range Experiment Station, Fort Collins, CO.

LOCATION: AZ

KEYWORDS: HERPETOFAUNA, WILDLIFE

ABSTRACT

Data on reptiles and amphibians were gathered using pit-fall traps and by observation along the Gila River northeast of Florence, Pinal County, Arizona. Four habitat types were sampled: desert wash, desert upland, mature salt cedar, and mesquite bosque. A total of 104 individuals of 12 species were trapped and an additional seven species were observed. Based on trap data, species diversity was greatest in the desert wash, and lowest in the salt cedar habitat. Reptiles and amphibians showed little use of the salt cedar habitat which may reflect the lack of structural diversity in the herbaceous and shrub layers and reduced light penetration due to a dense canopy.

Johnson, R.R., and D.A. Jones, tech. coord. 1977. Importance, preservation, and management of riparian habitat: A symposium. US Dep. Agric. For. Serv. Gen. Tech. Rep. RM-143, 217pp. Rocky Mountain Forest and Range Experiment Station, Fort Collins, CO. 80521

LOCATION: WESTERN U.S.

KEYWORDS: ENDANGERED SPECIES HABITAT, AQUATIC ECOSYSTEMS

ABSTRACT

Twelve presented and 15 contributed papers highlighting what is known about this unique, diminishing vegetative type: characteristics, classification systems, associated fauna, use conflicts, management alternatives, and research needs. Speakers stressed the continuity and interrelationships of riparian ecosystems, their wildlife and vegetation, historic and current uses.

Johnson, R.R., and J.F. McCormick, tech. coord. 1978. Strategies for protection and management of floodplain wetlands and other riparian ecosystems. Proc. Symp. Callaway Gardens, GA. U.S. Dep. Agric. For. Serv. Gen. Tech. Rep. WO-12, Washington DC. 410pp.

LOCATION: U.S.

KEYWORDS: FLOODPLAIN, WETLANDS

ABSTRACT

The proceedings consists of 55 invited, contributed and poster-session papers presented in three basic sessions: characteristics, values, and management of floodplain wetlands and other riparian ecosystems. The management session includes position papers by the Environmental Protection Agency, Forest Service, Fish and Wildlife Service, Soil Conservation Service and Bureau of Land Management.

Johnson, R.R., and L.T. Haight. 1985. Avian use of xeroriparian ecosystems in the North American warm deserts. Pages 156-160 in Riparian Ecosystems and Their Management: Reconciling Conflicting Uses. Proceedings of the Symposium. US Dep. Agric. For. Serv. Gen. Tech. Rep. RM-120, 523pp. Rocky Mountain Forest and Range Experiment Station, Fort Collins, CO.

LOCATION: AZ

KEYWORDS: XERORIPARIAN, RIPARIAN BIRDS, WARM DESERTS

ABSTRACT

Results of xeroriparian avian censuses are compared with paired desert upland censuses for various sub-divisions of the Sonoran Desert. With few exceptions xeroriparian habitat supports 5 to 10 times the population densities and species diversity of surrounding desert uplands.

Johnson, R.R., and C.H. Lowe. 1985. On the development of riparian ecology. Pages 112-116 in Riparian Ecosystems and Their Management: Reconciling Conflicting Uses. Proceedings of the Symposium. US Dep. Agric. For. Serv. Gen. Tech. Rep. RM-120, 523pp. Rocky Mountain Forest and Range Experiment Station, Fort Collins, CO.

LOCATION: U.S.

KEYWORDS: RIPARIAN ECOLOGY

ABSTRACT

The peculiarly western development of riparian ecology in North America is examined. Gradients in riparian systems are discussed with regard to transriparian and intrariparian continua, including xeroriparian communities. Consistent with the fact that riparian lands are technically wetlands, Aquatic, Riparian, and Terrestrial systems harbor peculiarly obligate species structured into distinctive biotic communities throughout all of North America.

Johnson, R.R., C.D. Ziebell, D.R. Patton, P.F. Ffolliott, and R.H. Hamre. tech. coords. 1985. In Riparian Ecosystems and Their Management: Reconciling Conflicting Uses. Proceedings of the Symposium. US Dep. Agric. For. Serv. Gen. Tech. Rep. RM-120, 523pp. Rocky Mountain Forest and Range Experiment Station, Fort Collins, CO.

LOCATION: U.S., WORLD WIDE

KEYWORDS: RECREATION, AGRICULTURE, WILDLIFE LIVESTOCK USE

ABSTRACT

These proceedings include 105 papers and 12 poster presentations. Topics include: physical characteristics, hydrology, and ecology of riparian ecosystems; riparian resources: recreation, agriculture, wildlife, livestock use, fisheries, and amphibians and reptiles; multiple-use planning and management; legal and institutional needs; riparian ecosystems in dryland zones of the world.

Johnson, S.R., H.L. Gary, and Stanley L. Ponce. 1978. Range cattle impacts on stream water quality in the Colorado Front Range. US Dep. Agric. For. Serv. Res. Note RM 359, Rocky Mountain Forest and Range Experiment Station. Fort Collins, CO. 8pp.

LOCATION: CO

KEYWORDS: GRAZING IMPACTS, WATER QUALITY, PATHOGENIC BACTERIA

ABSTRACT

Studies on two adjacent pastures along Trout Creek in Central Colorado indicated only minor effects of cattle grazing on water quality. Bacterial contamination of the water, however, significantly increased. Following removal of the cattle, bacterial counts dropped to levels similar to those in the ungrazed pasture.

Jones, K.B., and P.G. Glinski. 1985. Microhabitats of lizards in a
southwestern riparian community. Pages 342-346 in Riparian
Ecosystems and Their Management: Reconciling Conflicting Uses.
Proceedings of the Symposium. US Dep. Agric. For. Serv. Gen. Tech.
Rep. RM-120, 523pp. Rocky Mountain Forest and Range Experiment
Station, Fort Collins, CO.

LOCATION: AZ

KEYWORDS: LIZARDS, RIPARIAN COMMUNITY, MICROHABITATS

ABSTRACT

Relationships between lizard abundance and distribution, and
certain selected microhabitats were determined for a southwestern
riparian community. Distribution of lizards in riparian habitat
appear to reflect availability of preferred habitats; certain lizards
and microhabitats were widespread while others were limited to small
portions of the study area. Patterns of lizard distribution in
microhabitats are discussed.

Kauffman, J.B., W.C. Krueger, and M. Vavra. 1983. Impacts of cattle on
streambanks in northeastern Oregon. J. of Range Manage.
36(6):683-685.

LOCATION: OR

KEYWORDS: GRAZING IMPACTS, STREAMBANKS

ABSTRACT

Impacts of a late season livestock grazing strategy on streambank
erosion, morphology, and undercutting were studied for 2 years along
Catherine Creek in northeastern Oregon. Streambank loss,
disturbance, and undercutting were compared between grazing
treatments, vegetation type, and stream-meander position. No
significant differences were found among vegetation types or
stream-meander location. Significantly greater streambank erosion
and disturbance occurred in grazed areas than in exclosed areas
during the 1978 and 1979 grazing periods. Over-winter erosion was
not significantly different among treatments. However, erosion
related to livestock grazing and trampling was enough to create
significantly greater annual streambank losses when compared to
ungrazed areas.

Kauffman, J.B., and W.C. Krueger. 1984. Livestock impacts on riparian ecosystems and streamside management implications...A review. J. of Range Manage. 37(5):430-437.

LOCATION: WESTERN U.S.

KEYWORDS: GRAZING IMPACTS, STREAMSIDE MANAGEMENT, WILDLIFE, RECREATION, FISHERIES

ABSTRACT

This paper reviews 100 papers dealing with the impacts of grazing upon riparian ecosystems. Conclusions are: public lands must be managed on a true multiple use basis that recognizes and evaluates the biological potential of each ecological zone in relation to the present and future needs of our society as a whole. Management strategies that recognize all resource values must be designated to maintain or restore the integrity of riparian communities.

Keller, C.R., and K.P. Burnham. 1982. Riparian fencing, grazing, and trout habitat preference on Summit Creek, Idaho. N. Am. J. of Fish. Manage. 2:53-59.

LOCATION: ID

KEYWORDS: RIPARIAN FENCING, GRAZING, TROUT HABITAT PREFERENCE

ABSTRACT

In 1975, 3.2 km of Summit Creek, Idaho were fenced by the Bureau of Land Management to exclude livestock from the riparian area. Six stream sections were electrofished in 1979 to determine differences in trout abundance, size, and growth between grazed and ungrazed stream sections. Electrofishing stations were paired by habitat type. There were more trout in ungrazed sections than in grazed sections in all three habitat types sampled. With one exception, there were more catchable-sized (200 mm long or longer) rainbow trout (Salmo gairdneri) an brook trout (Salvelinus foninalis) in the ungrazed area than in the grazed area. There was also evidence that the average size of the fish was less in grazed sections.

Kindschy, R.R. 1985. Response of red willow to beaver use in south-eastern Oregon. J. Wildl. Manage. 49(1):26-28.

LOCATION: OR

KEYWORDS: <u>RED WILLOW, BEAVER, GRAZING IMPACTS</u>

ABSTRACT

Red willow (<u>Salix lasiandra</u>) is a common willow species that assumes tree form in the riparian communities of western North America. Utilization by herbivores has reduced or entirely eliminated willow and other riparian tree species, such as alder (<u>Alnus tenuifolia</u>), aspen (<u>Populus tremuloides</u>), and cottonwood (<u>P. trichocarpa</u>), from many otherwise suitable habitats in the western United States.

Knight, A.W., and R.L. Bottorff. 1984. The importance of riparian vegetation to stream ecosystems. Pages 160-167 <u>in</u> Riparian Ecosystems and Their Management: Reconciling Conflicting Uses. Proceedings of the Symposium. US Dep. Agric. For. Serv. Gen. Tech. Rep. RM-120, 523pp. Rocky Mountain Forest and Range Experiment Station, Fort Collins, CO.

LOCATION: CA

KEYWORDS: <u>RIPARIAN VEGETATION, STREAM ECOSYSTEMS, AQUATIC INVERTEBRATES</u>

ABSTRACT

Riparian vegetation is very important in determining the structure and function of stream ecosystems. Most aquatic organisms, both invertebrates and fish, are directly or indirectly dependent on inputs of terrestrial detritus to the stream for their food. Natural changes in riparian vegetation and the biotic processing of detritus, as well as other factors, determine the kinds of abundance of aquatic invertebrates living in streams, from headwaters to large rivers. Removal of riparian vegetation will significantly affect stream organisms by: 1) decreasing detrital (food) inputs; 2) increasing the potential for primary production in aquatic plants; 3) increasing summer water temperatures; 4) changing water quality and quantity; and 5) decreasing terrestrial habitat for adult insects.

Knopf, F.L. 1985. Significance of riparian vegetation to breeding birds across an altitudinal cline. Pages 105-111 in Riparian Ecosystems and Their Management: Reconciling Conflicting Uses. Proceedings of the Symposium. US Dep. Agric. For. Serv. Gen. Tech. Rep. RM-120, 523pp. Rocky Mountain Forest and Range Experiment Station, Fort Collins, CO.

LOCATION: CO

KEYWORDS: RIPARIAN VEGETATION, BREEDING BIRDS, ALTITUDINAL CLINE

ABSTRACT

The relative significance of riparian zones to breeding birds was documented at 6 elevations between 1,200 and 2,750 m in the Platte River drainage of the Colorado Front Range. Bird communities were inventoried during 1,440 10-min surveys at points in riparian and upland vegetation on the 6 study areas during May and June 1981-1982. Totals of 124 and 111 species were observed on the 6 study areas during the 2 years; 82% of all species were observed in riparian sites than in uplands. Riparian bird communities were simplistically structured at high elevations and most complex at lower elevations; upland communities were more complex at higher elevations. Higher diversity analyses indicated that riparian sites at the lowest and highest elevations are most significant to a regional avifauna. Management actions to enhance avian communities in western states should place primary emphasis on riparian zones at low elevations, secondary emphasis on those at the highest elevations, and de-emphasize efforts at intermediate elevations.

Krausman, P.R., K.R. Rautenstrauch, and B.D. Leopold. 1985. Xeroriparian systems used by desert mule deer in Texas and Arizona. Pages 144-149 in Riparian Ecosystems and Their Management: Reconciling Conflicting Uses. Proceedings of the Symposium. US Dep. Agric. For. Serv. Gen. Tech. Rep. RM-120, 523pp. Rocky Mountain Forest and Range Experiment Station, Fort Collins, CO.

LOCATION: AZ, TX

KEYWORDS: MULE DEER, XERORIPARIAN SYSTEMS

ABSTRACT

We examined desert mule deer (Odocoileus hemionus crooki) occurrance in xeroriparian systems in Arizona and Texas. Most deer in Arizona were located in washes. Most deer in Texas were located between washes. Xeroriparian areas are important habitat components for desert mule deer when they provide forage, thermal cover and travel lanes.

Krueger, H.O., and S.H. Anderson. 1985. The use of cattle as a management tool for wildlife in shrub-willow riparian systems. Pages 300-304. in Riparian Ecosystems and Their Management: Reconciling Conflicting Uses. Proceedings of the Symposium. US Dep. Agric. For. Serv. Gen. Tech. Rep. RM-120, 523pp. Rocky Mountain Forest and Range Experiment Station, Fort Collins, CO.

LOCATION: WY

KEYWORDS: SHRUB-WILLOW RIPARIAN SYSTEMS, LIVESTOCK GRAZING

ABSTRACT

In high altitude shrub-willow riparian systems cattle can have a beneficial effect on wildlife by creating tunnels throughout the habitat. Mean tunnel heights for two study areas were 0.75 and 0.95 m with 41% of the shrubs sampled forming tunnels in each study area. These tunnels benefit birds and mammals by opening up willows which in turn increases the grassland habitat and structural diversity of vegetation.

Lea, G.D. 1979. BLM Management and policy for riparian/stream ecosystems. Pages 13-15 in Cope, O.B. ed. Grazing and Riparian/Stream Ecosystems: Proceedings of the Forum. Trout Unlimited Inc., Denver, CO. 94pp.

LOCATION: U.S.

KEYWORDS: RIPARIAN MANAGEMENT POLICY, INVENTORY OF PUBLIC LANDS

REVIEWER'S ABSTRACT

Federal management policies of the Bureau of Land Management for riparian vegetation are discussed. Mandates of the Federal Land Management Policy Act of 1976 effectively sets the scene for recognition and management of riparian values. Section 102(A) (2) establishes policy for the systematic inventory of public lands.

Lloyd, J. 1985. COWFISH: Habitat capability model. Wildlife and Fish Habitat Relationship Program, Northern Region, US Dep. Agric. For. Serv., P.O. Box 7669, Missoula, MT 59807. 32pp.

LOCATION: MT

KEYWORDS: GRAZING MANAGEMENT, FISHERIES, STREAM INVENTORY, RIPARIAN INVENTORY, MODELLING

ABSTRACT

The Habitat Capability Model is patterned after the U.S. Fish and Wildlife Service's Habitat Suitability Index. The HCM translates the HSI values into actual animal numbers or values. In the HCM the HSI value (0.0 - 1.0) is a secondary output. The model predicts the effects the past and present grazing system may have on the fisheries environment.

Lowe, C.H. 1985. Amphibians and reptiles in southwest riparian ecosystems. Pages 339-341 in Riparian Ecosystems and Their Management: Reconciling Conflicting Uses. Proceedings of the Symposium. US Dep. Agric. For. Serv. Gen. Tech. Rep. RM-120, 523pp. Rocky Mountain Forest and Range Experiment Station, Fort Collins, CO.

LOCATION: AZ

KEYWORDS: AMPHIBIANS, REPTILES, OBLIGATE RIPARIAN SPECIES

ABSTRACT

Obligate riparian amphibians and reptiles in Arizona and Sonora, Mexico are dicussed. Local population extinctions in Arizona are examined. Special status for obligate riparian species is proposed.

MacCracken, J.G., D.W. Uresk, and R.M. Hansen. 1985. Rodent-vegetation relationships in southeastern Montana. Northwest Science 59(4):272-278.

LOCATION: MT

KEYWORDS: RODENTS, GRASSLAND, RIPARIAN COMMUNITY, SAGEBRUSH COMMUNITY, RODENT ABUNDANCE

ABSTRACT

Plant communities of southeastern Montana were surveyed for rodents over a two-year period. Grassland, riparian, and sagebrush communities showed the greatest rodent abundance and species diversity. There was a significant positive relationship between rodent abundance and the cover provided by some understory plant species and tree density on the study area.

Mahoney, D.L., and D.C. Erman. 1984. The role of streamside bufferstrips in the ecology of aquatic biota. Pages 168-176 in California Riparian Systems: Ecology, Conservation, and Productive Management, Warner, Richard E. and K. Hendrix eds. 1035pp. University of California Press, Berkely, CA.

LOCATION: CA

KEYWORDS: <u>BUFFERSTRIPS, RIPARIAN VEGETATION, STREAM ORGANISMS, LOGGING, STREAM SEDIMENT</u>

ABSTRACT

Riparian vegetation is important as a source of food to stream organisms, as shade over small-order streams, and as a bank-stabilizing force to prevent excessive sedimentation and to intercept pollutants. Logging may significantly affect each of these factors unless proper protective measures are employed. Current research is underway on the recovery of small northern California streams after logging. Analysis of algal samples from 30 streams shows light intensity and chlorophyll concentrations are major factors related to logging intensity that affect instream primary production. Transportable sediment from 24 streambeds has shown that this measure of sediment is higher (P = .001) in logged and narrow buffered streams than in controls 7 to 10 years after logging.

Marlow, C.B., and T.M. Pogacnik. 1986. Time of grazing and cattle-induced damage to streambanks. Pages 279-284 in Riparian Ecosystems and Their Management: Reconciling Conflicting Uses. Proceedings of the Symposium. US Dep. Agric. For. Serv. Gen. Tech. Rep. RM-120, 523pp. Rocky Mountain Forest and Range Experiment Station, Fort Collins, CO.

LOCATION: MT

KEYWORDS: <u>RIPARIAN COMMUNITIES, SOIL MOISTURE, RIPARIAN ZONE, GRAZING IMPACT, TRAMPLING</u>

ABSTRACT

Cattle impact riparian communities through two processes: grazing and trampling. Re-evaluation of management practices indicates that implementation of rest rotation grazing management and limiting cattle use of riparian vegetation to 20% of the standing crop will reduce impact. Rest rotation and light grazing may improve plant vigor but little information is available on how well either practice controls bank damage from trampling. A three-year grazing study in southwestern Montana indicates that the level of cattle use in the riparian zone has little bearing on streambank damage (r^2=0.06). Soil moisture content directly affects (r^2=0.85) the streambanks susceptibility to trampling. Postponing or deferring grazing until streambanks have dried (10% soil moisture) will further protect the riparian zone from damage.

Marlow, C.B., and T.M. Pogacnik. 1986. Cattle feeding and resting patterns in a foothills riparian zone. J. of Range Manage. 39(3):212-216.

KEYWORDS: GRAZING, FOOTHILLS RIPARIAN ZONE, SEASONAL FEEDING PATTERNS IN RIPARIAN AREAS

ABSTRACT

Cattle impact on riparian areas is dependent upon both their behavior and utilization of streamside vegetation. Development of grazing strategies for riparian environments would be enhanced by and understanding of cattle behavior in riparian and adjacent uplands. Results of a 2-year study indicate that a seasonal trend in cattle use of riparian and upland areas exists. Unless low precipitation limited upland forage quality/production, cattle spent a siginficant (P 0.05) occurred in the riparian zone from late August through September. Resting patterns differed only during the early part of the grazing season when cattle spent significantly more (0.5) of their time resting in upland areas.

Martin, K.E. 1984. Recreation planning as a tool to restore and protect riparian systems. Pages 748-757 in California Riparian Systems: Ecology, Conservation, and Productive Management, Warner, R.E. and K. Hendrix eds. 1035pp. University of California Press, Berkeley, CA.

LOCATION: CA

KEYWORDS: RECREATION

ABSTRACT

This paper examines planning strategies which assures the protection of riparian systems while providing for recreation use. A riparian forest adjacent to a densely populated area and subject to intensive recreation use is investigated. The popular recreation activities that occur in connection with a riparian system are identified and methods for controlling recreation use are discussed.

McCluskey, D.C. 1983. Willow planting for riparian habitat improvement. US Dep. Inter., Bur. Land Manage. Tech. Note 363 Federal Center, Bldg. 50, Printed Materials Distribution Center, Denver, CO 80225-0047. 21pp.

LOCATION: UT

KEYWORDS: WILLOW PLANTING, REVEGETATION, HABITAT IMPROVEMENT

ABSTRACT

This report is designed for field personnel who are interested in employing willow (Salix spp.) planting as a technique for riparian habitat improvement. While other methods are available which utilize seedlings or tube packs, the technique discussed here will only deal with vegetative cuttings of willows because they are, for many areas, the easiest to obtain, lowest in cost, usually locally acclimated and produce a good benefit/cost ratio for the project.

Meehan, W.R., and W.S. Platts. 1981. Influence of forest and rangeland management on anadromous fish habitat in Western North America. US Dep. Agric. For. Serv. Gen Tech. Rep. PNW-124, Pacific Northwest Forest and Range Experiment Station. Portland, OR. 25pp.

LOCATION: WESTERN U.S.

KEYWORDS: GRAZING, RANGE MANAGEMENT, FISH HABITAT

ABSTRACT

This paper documents current knowledge on interactions of livestock and fish habitat. Included are discussions of incompatibility and compatibility between livestock grazing and fisheries, present management guidelines, information needed for problem solving, information available for problem solving, and future research needs.

Moore, E., E. Janes, F. Kinsinger, K. Pitney, and J. Sainsbury. 1979. Livestock grazing management and water quality protection-State of the art reference document. EPA, Water Div., 1200 6th Ave. Seattle, WA 98101; EPA Water Div., 1860 Lincoln, Denver, CO 80203; US Dep. Inter., Bur. Land Manage., Federal Center, Denver, CO 80225. 174pp.

LOCATION: WESTERN U.S.

KEYWORDS: WATER QUALITY, LIVESTOCK GRAZING, POLLUTION NONPOINT SOURCE, BEST MANAGEMENT PRACTICES

ABSTRACT

The report is a state of the art reference of methods, procedures and practices or methods suitable for preventing or minimizing water quality impacts, and alternatives for the assessment of a rangeland watershed's total runoff and pollution production.

Moring, J.R., G.C. Garman, and D.M. Mullen. 1985. The value of riparian zones for protecting aquatic systems: General concerns and recent studies in Maine. Pages 315-319 in Riparian Ecosystems and Their Management: Reconciling Conflicting Uses. Proceedings of the Symposium. US Dep. Agric. For. Serv. Gen. Tech. Rep. RM-120, 523pp. Rocky Mountain Forest and Range Experiment Station, Fort Collins, CO.

LOCATION: ME

KEYWORDS: VEGETATION ALTERATION

ABSTRACT

Riparian zones serve important functions for fisheries and aquatic systems: shading, bank stability, prevention of excess sedimentation, overhanging cover for fishes, and energy input from invertebrates and allochthonous material. Impacts from loss of riparian areas are discussed in relation to aquatic ecosystems, and the results of two recent studies in Maine are reviewed.

Odum, E.P. 1978. Ecological importance of the riparian zone. Pages 2-4 in Strategies for Protection and Management of Floodplain Wetlands and Other Riparian Ecosystems. Johnson, R.R. and J.F. McCormick, tech. coords. Proc. Symp. Callaway Gardens, GA. US Dep. Agric. For. Serv. Gen. Tech. Rep. WO-12. Washington DC. 410pp.

LOCATION: U.S.

KEYWORDS: RIPARIAN ZONE FUNCTION

ABSTRACT

Riparian zones have their greatest value as buffers and filters between man's urban and agricultural development and his most vital life support - water. Preservation based on public riparian rights provide an effective hedge against overdevelopment of urgan sprawl and agricultural or forest monoculture.

Ohmart, R.D., B.W. Anderson, and W.C. Hunter. 1985. Influence of agriculture on waterbird, wader, and shorebird use along the lower Colorado River. Pages 117-122 in Riparian Ecosystems and Their Management: Reconciling Conflicting Uses. Proceedings of the Symposium. US Dep. Agric. For. Serv. Gen. Tech. Rep. RM-120, 523pp. Rocky Mountain Forest and Range Experiment Station, Fort Collins, CO.

LOCATION: AZ, CA

KEYWORDS: AGRICULTURE, WATERBIRD, WADING BIRDS, SHOREBIRD

ABSTRACT

Waterbird, wader, and shorebird use of the Colorado River was restricted to habitats in or immediately adjacent to the river prior to agricultural development. We studied agricultural habitats systematically for three years and identified those agricultural settings that were most important for individual species and groups of waterbirds, waders, and shorebirds.

Parker, M., F.J. Wood, B.H. Smith, and R.G. Elder. 1985. Erosional downcutting in lower order riparian ecosystems: Have historical changes been caused by removal of beaver? Pages 35-38 in Riparian Ecosystems and Their Management: Reconciling Conflicting Uses. Proceedings of the Symposium. US Dep. Agric. For. Serv. Gen. Tech. Rep. RM-120, 523pp. Rocky Mountain Forest and Range Experiment Station, Fort Collins, CO.

LOCATION: WY

KEYWORDS: BEAVER, DOWNCUTTING

ABSTRACT

Streams often are described as being in a state of dynamic equilibrium. We hypothesize that, in lower order streams, beaver may be able to resist perturbations to this equilibrium if the perturbations are not too great. After suggesting the thermodynamic and mechanistic bases, we propose a simple model by which the potential of beaver to resist perturbations can be quantified. The model accounts for many common observations, and appears applicable to a variety of management problems.

Platts, W.S. 1979. Livestock grazing and riparian/stream ecosystems--An overview. Pages 39-45 in Cope, O.B. ed. Grazing and Riparian/Stream Ecosystems: Proceedings of the Forum. Trout Unlimited Inc., Denver, CO. 94pp.

LOCATION: WESTERN U.S.

KEYWORDS: GRAZING IMPACTS, STREAM MANAGEMENT

ABSTRACT

Livestock grazing can affect all four components of the aquatic system--streamside vegetation, stream channel morphology, shape and quality of the water column, and the structure of the soil portion of the streambank. Livestock grazing can affect the streamside environment by changing, reducing, or eliminating vegetation bordering the stream. Channel morphology can be changed by sediment accrual, altered channel substratecomposition, disrupted pool-riffle relationships, and channel widening. Livestock can trample streambanks causing banks to slough off, creating flase setback banks, and exposing banks to accelerated soil erosion.

Platts, W.S. 1981. Sheep and cattle grazing strategies on riparian-stream environments. Pages 252-270 in Proceedings of the Wildlife-Livestock Relationships Symposium: Univ. of Idaho, Forest, Wildlife and Range Experiment Station, Moscow, ID.

LOCATION: WESTERN U.S.

KEYWORDS: SHEEP GRAZING, CATTLE GRAZING

ABSTRACT

Research studies involving the effects of cattle and sheep grazing strategies on stream riparian habitat are discussed. Initial results indicate that herded sheep grazing may have little effect on streams and the riparian environment. The effects of cattle grazing first appear on the streambanks and riparian vegetation. Habitat alteration occurs at utilization rates of 65% or more, and alteration is insignificant when utilization is less than 25 percent. Continued research is needed to identify grazing strategies compatible with riparian environments, and to develop new grazing strategies.

Platts, W.S. 1981. Protection and enhancement of Pacific salmonids on ranges grazed by livestock: An overview. Pages 62-65 in Hassler, T.J. ed. Proceedings: Propagation, Enhancement, and Rehabilitation of Anadromous Salmonid Populations and Habitat in the Pacific Northwest Symposium. Humboldt State University, California Cooperative Fishery Research Unit, Arcata, CA.

LOCATION: WESTERN U.S.

KEYWORDS: GRAZING IMPACTS, GRAZING STRATEGY

ABSTRACT

When European man arrived on the Pacific Coast, the streams were teaming with salmonids in a natural environment. Since the mid-1800s, a decline in the quality of the salmonid habitat has occurred. One land use responsible for part of this decline has been improper grazing by both sheep and cattle. The solutions that will reverse this decline rest with range and fishery specialists, who must coordinate their studies and tackle the riparian issue together. They must determine the suitability of each habitat type for grazing, and the correct grazing strategy with proper animal distribution.

Platts, W.S. 1982. Livestock and riparian-fishery interactions: What are the facts? Trans. of the 47th N. Am. Wildlife and Natural Resources Conference. 47:507-515 Wildlife Management Institute, Washington, DC.

LOCATION: WESTERN U.S.

KEYWORDS: GRAZING-FISHERY INTERACTIONS

ABSTRACT

Land managers are having a tough enough time trying to properly manage the riparian-stream habitats without the literature confusing their thinking. This report attempts to evaluate past findings and to place the facts in better perspective. Many articles in the literature discuss the effects of livestock grazing on riparian-fishery habitats, but most are either intuitively developed or are a state-of-the-art reports that do not include actual data for analysis.

Platts, W.S., W.F. Megahan, G.W. Minshall. 1983. Methods for evaluating stream, riparian, and biotic conditions. US Dep. Agric. For. Serv. Gen. Tech. Rep. INT-138. Intermountain Forest and Range Experiment Station, Ogden, UT. 70pp.

LOCATION: WESTERN U.S.

KEYWORDS: AQUATIC HABITAT, FISH, STREAMS, INVENTORY

ABSTRACT

This report develops a standard way of measuring stream, riparian,and biotic conditions and evaluates the validity of the measurements recommended. Accuracy and precision of most measurements are defined. This report will be of value to those persons documenting, monitoring, or predicting stream conditions and their biotic resources, especially those related to impacts from land uses.

Platts, W.S. 1984. Riparian system/livestock grazing interaction research in the intermountain west. Pages 424-429 in California Riparian Systems: Ecology, Conservation, and Productive Management, Warner, R.E. and K. Hendrix eds. 1035pp. University of California Press, Berkeley, CA.

LOCATION: INTERMOUNTAIN WEST

KEYWORDS: RESEARCH, GRAZING

ABSTRACT

Research which identifies the influences livestock grazing has on riparian and aquatic ecosystems is limited. A research study initiated in 1975 by the USDA Forest Service is studying these influences and finding solutions so managers will have better information to evaluate rang management alternatives. Preliminary findings on continuous and rest-rotation grazing systems are discussed.

Platts, W.S., K.A. Gebhardt, and W.L. Jackson. 1985. The effects of large storm events on Basin-Range riparian stream habitats. Pages 30-34 in Riparian Ecosystems and Their Management: Reconciling Conflicting Uses. Proceedings of the Symposium. US Dep. Agric. For. Serv. Gen. Tech. Rep. RM-120, 523pp. Rocky Mountain Forest and Range Experiment Station, Fort Collins, CO.

LOCATION: NV, UT

KEYWORDS: STORM EVENTS, FLOODING, UNGRAZED RIPARIAN, GRAZED RIPARIAN

ABSTRACT

Large storm events had major impacts on stream riparian reaches that had received heavy livestock grazing. One ungrazed rehabilitated stream reach actually improved in habitat condition while the two adjacent grazed stream reaches decreased. Each stream reacted differently to channel erosion, with two streams showing mainly lateral channel movement and the third stream vertical channel movement.

Platts, W.S., and R.L. Nelson. 1985. Stream habitat and fisheries response to livestock grazing and instream improvement structures, Big Creek, Utah. J. of Soil and Water Cons. 40(4):374-379.

LOCATION: UT

KEYWORDS: STREAM HABITAT, LIVESTOCK GRAZING, STREAM IMPROVEMENT

ABSTRACT

Fisheries habitat and fisheries response were compared on an area protected from grazing for 11 years and on adjacent, heavily grazed areas of similar structural and riparian character. Prohibiting grazing dramatically improved riparian vegetation, streambanks, and stream channel conditions. But this improvement was countered by off-site upstream influences and on-site instream improvement structures that function as fine sediment traps. Fish population did not respond to improving habitat conditions because the relatively small size of the livestock exclosure did not reduce incoming, limiting influences created by upstream conditions and the artificial nature of the fishery.

Platts, W.S., and R.L. Nelson. 1985. Streamside and upland vegetation use by cattle. J. of Rangelands. 7(4):5-7.

LOCATION: WESTERN U.S.

KEYWORDS: GRAZING, STREAMSIDE VEGETATION, CATTLE USE

ABSTRACT

In the Western United States, some streams no longer have their once productive streamside vegetal cover. A century of heavy grazing on these riparian zones has caused cumulative impacts to streambanks that have resulted in the transformation of many riparian habitats from a dominant growth of trees to brush to forb. Inadequate animal drinking water on upland areas and preference for streamside vegetation have been traditionally important factors causing streamside corridors to be more heavily grazed than are other rangeland areas.

Platts, W.S., and R.L. Nelson. 1985. Will the riparian pasture build good streams? J. of Rangelands. 7(4)7-11.

LOCATION: WESTERN U.S.

KEYWORDS: RIPARIAN PASTURE, GRAZING

ABSTRACT

Since the mid 1930s, improved range management practices have steadily enhanced the deteriorated rangelands that existed at that time. Although overall rangeland conditions have continually improved, riparian range sites (lands supporting vegetation that requires free or unbound water or moist soils) have not necessarily followed suit. Many riparian areas remain in a deteriorated state because they fail to respond favorably to the management strategies being applied to the allotment.

Platts, W.S., and J.N Rinne. 1985. Riparian and stream enhancement management and research in the Rocky Mountains. N. Am. J. of Fish. Manage. 5:115-125.

LOCATION: ROCKY MOUNTAIN STATES

KEYWORDS: RESEARCH NEEDS, RIPARIAN

ABSTRACT

This report reviews past stream enhancement research in the Rocky Mountains, its adequacy, and research that should be done to improve the effectiveness of future stream enhancement projects. Research is lacking on stream improvement in a watershed context on a long-term basis. Not all streams can be enhanced. Enhancement should be attempted only after techniques described in the literature have been carefully considered and judged appropriate for the selected site.

Prichard, D.E., and L.L. Upham. 1986. Texas creek riparian enhancement study. N. Am. Wildl. and Nat. Res. Conf. 47:

LOCATION: CO

KEYWORDS: STREAM IMPROVEMENT, GRAZING IMPACT, RIPARIAN IMPROVEMENT, STREAM IMPROVEMENT, REVEGETATION

A riparian habitat enhancement study was conducted on Texas Creek, a small cold water stream in south central Colorado on public land administered by the Bureau of Land Management. The objective was to quantitatively measure responses in riparian vegetation, channel provile, and fish population resulting from manipulation of livestock and selected treatments i.e., gabions, plantings, and stream bank stabilization. A one-half mile (0.8 km) portion of Texas Creek was divided into three study segments. Segment A represented deferred seasonal livestock grazing with no habitat manipulation treatments. Segment B excluded livestock grazing with intensive habitat treatments. Segment C excluded livestock grazing with no habitat mainpulations.

Richards, M.T., and A.B. Wood. 1985. The economic value of sportfishing at Lees Ferry, Arizona. Pages 219-222 in Riparian Ecosystems and Their Management: Reconciling Conflicting Uses. Proceedings of the Symposium. US Dep. Agric. For. Serv. Gen. Tech. Rep. RM-120, 523pp. Rocky Mountain Forest and Range Experiment Station, Fort Collins, CO.

LOCATION: AZ

KEYWORDS: FISHERIES, SPORTFISHING ECONOMIC VALUE, RECREATION

ABSTRACT

Economic values were estimated for trophy and non-trophy anglers at Lees Ferry, Arizona. Management recommendations are made, based on these values, that permit discrimination between various users of the riparian environment and among anglers specifically.

Rinne, J.N. 1985. Livestock grazing on southwestern streams: A complex research problem. Pages 295-299 in Riparian Ecosystems and Their Management: Reconciling Conflicting Uses. Proceedings of the Symposium. US Dep. Agric. For. Serv. Gen. Tech. Rep. RM-120, 523pp. Rocky Mountain Forest and Range Experiment Station, Fort Collins, CO.

LOCATION: NM

KEYWORDS: GRAZING IMPACT, RESEARCH

ABSTRACT

Conducting viable research on the effects of domestic livestock grazing on stream environments and biota in southwestern National Forests is problematic. The multiple-use concept, spatial temporal factors, inadequate control and replication, and changes in land management objectives and direction render it difficult to effectively study grazing impacts.

Rosgen, D.L. 1985. A stream classification system. Pages 91-95 in Riparian Ecosystems and Their Management: Reconciling Conflicting Uses. Proceedings of the Symposium. US Dep. Agric. For. Serv. Gen. Tech. Rep. RM-120, 523pp. Rocky Mountain Forest and Range Experiment Station, Fort Collins, CO.

LOCATION: WESTERN U.S.

KEYWORDS: STREAM CLASSIFICATION

ABSTRACT

A stream classification system is presented which categorizes various stream types by morphological characteristics. Delineation criteria are stream gradient, sinuosity, width/depth ratio, channel materials, entrenchment, confinement, and soil/landform features. Applications include riparian management guidelines, fisheries habitat interpretations, hydraulic geometry and sediment transport relationships.

Schultze, R.F., and G.I. Wilcox. 1985. Emergency Measures for Streambank stabilization: An evaluation. Pages 59-61 in Riparian Ecosystems and Their Management: Reconciling Conflicting Uses. Proceedings of the Symposium. US Dep. Agric. For. Serv. Gen. Tech. Rep. RM-120, 523pp. Rocky Mountain Forest and Range Experiment Station, Fort Collins, CO.

LOCATION: CA

KEYWORDS: STREAMBANK STABILIZATION, REVEGETATION, FLOODING

ABSTRACT

Severe storms of 1978 through 1983 caused considerable damage to streams in California. The Soil Conservation Service used several mechanical and revegetation techniques to stabilize streambanks and re-establish riparian vegetation. Results of evaluations made on 29 projects are discussed and recommendations made to improve success.

Siekert, R.E., Q.D. Skinner, M.A. Smith, J.L. Dodd, J.D. Rogers. 1985. Channel response of an ephemeral stream in Wyoming to selected grazing treatments. Pages 276-278 in Riparian Ecosystems and Their Management: Reconciling Conflicting Uses. Proceedings of the Symposium. US Dep. Agric. For. Serv. Gen. Tech. Rep. RM-120, 523pp. Rocky Mountain Forest and Range Experiment Station, Fort Collins, CO.

LOCATION: WY

KEYWORDS: STREAM EPHEMERAL, GRAZING IMPACTS, STREAM-CHANNEL MORPHOLOGY

ABSTRACT

Studies of the effects of seasonal grazing on ephemeral stream morphology are summarized. Results indicate that spring grazing has no significant effect on channel morphology. Summer and fall grazing is associated with increases in channel cross-sectional area, with the degree of these impacts varying with climatic differences. Seasonal grazing can be used as a management tool for modifying channel morphology to promote channel stabilization.

Simcox, D.E., and E.H. Zube. 1985. Arizona riparian areas: A bibliography. University of Arizona, School of Natural Resources, Tucson, AZ. 38pp.

LOCATION: AZ, U.S.

KEYWORDS: HYDROLOGY, WILDLIFE, FISHERIES, ECONOMICS, LAW

ABSTRACT

381 bibliographic references related to riparian areas are listed. An extensive keyword index is included.

Short, H.L. 1985. Management goals and habitat structure. Pages 257-262 in Riparian Ecosystems and Their Management: Reconciling Conflicting Uses. Proceedings of the Symposium. US Dep. Agric. For. Serv. Gen. Tech. Rep. RM-120, 523pp. Rocky Mountain Forest and Range Experiment Station, Fort Collins, CO.

LOCATION: U.S.

KEYWORDS: WILDLIFE HABITAT STRUCTURE, RIPARIAN HABITATS

ABSTRACT

Many management goals can be developed for riparian habitats. Each goal may dictate different management policies, strategies, and tactics and result in different impacts on wildlife. Habitat structure, expressed in terms of habitat layers, can provide a useful framework for developing effective strategies for a variety of management goals because many different land uses can be associated with habitat layers. Well-developed goals are essential both for purposeful habitat management and for monitoring the impacts of different land uses on habitats.

Simons, L.H. 1985. Small mammal community structure in old growth and logged riparian habitat. Pages 505-506 in Riparian Ecosystems and Their Management: Reconciling Conflicting Uses. Proceedings of the Symposium. US Dep. Agric. For. Serv. Gen. Tech. Rep. RM-120, 523pp. Rocky Mountain Forest and Range Experiment Station, Fort Collins, CO.

LOCATION: CA

KEYWORDS: MAMMALS SMALL, TIMBER OLD GROWTH, LOGGING IMPACTS

ABSTRACT

Species richness and eveness were measured in small mammal communities from old growth and logged riparian habitat. Six species occurred in both habitats, while Clethrionomys occidentalis occupied only old growth. Similarities in understory vegetation, and proximity of old growth to the logged area, may promote similar communities in each habitat.

Sims, B.D., and L.D. Johnson. 1985. Structural anadromous fishery habitat improvement on the Siskiyou National Forest. Pages 502-504 in Riparian Ecosystems and Their Management: Reconciling Conflicting Uses. Proceedings of the Symposium. US Dep. Agric. For. Serv. Gen. Tech. Rep. RM-120, 523pp. Rocky Mountain Forest and Range Experiment Station, Fort Collins, CO.

LOCATION: OR

KEYWORDS: FOREST, FISHERY HABITAT STRUCTURE, FIS' 'NADROMOUS, STREAM IMPROVEMENT

ABSTRACT

Three separate strategies for allowing anadromous fish passage through culverts are discussed. These include: 1) construction of stepped log weirs to raise the pool level at the culvert outlet; 2) retrofitting circular culverts with a baffle system; and 3) use of an open-bottomed arch-type culvert. In addition, several log and gabion structures used to create pool habitat are discussed. All examples presented have survived several seasons and have achieved their fishery enhancement objectives.

Skovlin, J.K. 1984. Impacts of grazing on wetlands and riparian habitat: A review of our knowledge. Pages 1001-1103 in Developing Strategies for Rangeland Management. A report prepared by the committee on developing strategies for rangeland management. National Research Council/ National Academy of Sciences. Westview Press, Boulder, CO. 2022pp.

LOCATION: WESTERN U.S.

KEYWORDS: WETLAND GRAZING, GRAZING, GRAZING IMPACTS

ABSTRACT

This paper reviews impacts of grazing on wetland and riparian habitats throughout western North America. It identifies problems, discusses values and functions, and synthesizes study findings. Major topics are the effects of range livestock grazing on vegetation, watershed, and fish and wildlife. Specific subjects cover responses of (1) trees, shrubs, and herbaceous plants, (2) water quality, streambank stability, and features of upland erosion, and (3) large and small mammals, birds, and invertebrate organisms. Grazing strategies to improve habitats are proposed for better decisions in allocating riparian zone uses.

Stabler, D.F. 1985. Increasing summer flow in small streams through management of riparian areas and adjacent vegetation: A synthesis. Pages 206-210 in Riparian Ecosystems and Their Management: Reconciling Conflicting Uses. Proceedings of the Symposium. US Dep. Agric. For. Serv. Gen. Tech. Rep. RM-120, 523pp. Rocky Mountain Forest and Range Experiment Station, Fort Collins, CO.

LOCATION: WY

KEYWORDS: STREAM INCREASED SUMMER FLOW, HABITAT IMPROVEMENT

ABSTRACT

Construction of small dams, suppression of woody vegetation in and adjacent to riparian zones, and removal of livestock from streamsides have all led to summer streamflow increase. Potential may exist to manage small valley bottoms for summer flow increase, while maintaining or improving riparian habitat, range and watershed values.

Storch, R.L. 1979. Livestock/streamside management programs in eastern
Oregon. Pages 56-59 in Cope, O.B. ed. Grazing and Riparian/Stream
Ecosystems: Proceedings of the Forum. Trout Unlimited Inc., Denver,
Co. 94pp.

LOCATION: OR

KEYWORDS: GRAZING IMPACTS, STREAM EXCLOSURES

ABSTRACT

Uncontrolled livestock grazing has seriously affected the water
quality of stream throughout the country. Indiscriminate use of
streams by livestock results in breaking down the streambands, eating
and trampling shrubs that shade the streams and/or provide habitat
for wildlife, and disturbing the stream bottoms. The effects of such
use have been erosion of streambanks, higher water temperatures,
increased sedimentation, soil compaction, and reduction of the
quantity and quality of forage.

Stroup, W.W., and J. Stubbendieck. 1983. Multivariate statistical
methods to determine changes in botanical composition. J. of Range
Manage. 36(2):208-212.

LOCATION: U.S.

KEYWORDS: MULTIVARIATE STATISTICAL METHODS, BOTANICAL COMPOSITION

ABSTRACT

Confusion exists over the proper statistical methodology to use
in analyzing the effect of treatments on changes in botanical
composition over time. A rational for using multivariate statistics
is presented. Basic considerations involved in the use and
interpretation of multivariate statistics specifically appropriate to
the botanical composition problem are given. An example of how such
an analysis can be performed using a common statistical computing
package (SAS) is demonstrated.

Stuber, R.J. 1985. Trout habitat, abundance, and fishing opportunities in fenced v. unfenced riparian habitat along Sheep Creek, Colorado Pages 310-314 in Riparian Ecosystems and Their Management: Reconciling Conflicting Uses. Proceedings of the Symposium. US Dep. Agric. For. Serv. Gen. Tech. Rep. RM-120, 523pp. Rocky Mountain Forest and Range Experiment Station, Fort Collins, CO.

LOCATION: CO

KEYWORDS: RECREATION, TROUT HABITAT, FENCING, UNFENCED RIPARIAN AREAS

ABSTRACT

Fencing was used to protect 40 hectares of riparian stream habitat along 2.5 km of Sheep Creek, Colorado, from adverse impacts due to heavy streamside recreation use and cattle grazing. Fish habitat within the fenced area was narrower, deeper, and less streambank alteration, and better streamside vegetation than comparable unfenced sections. Estimated trout standing crop was twice as great, and proportional stock density (PSD) was higher than in unfenced sections. There was a higher proportion of nongame fish present in unfenced sections. Projected fishing opportunities within the fenced sections were double those estimated for a comparable length of unfenced habitat along the same stream.

Swank, G.W. Streamside management units in the Pacific Northwest. Pages 435-438 in Riparian Ecosystems and Their Management: Reconciling Conflicting Uses. Proceedings of the Symposium. US Dep. Agric. For. Serv. Gen. Tech. Rep. RM-120, 523pp. Rocky Mountain Forest and Range Experiment Station, Fort Collins, CO.

LOCATION: OR

KEYWORDS: STREAMSIDE MANAGEMENT UNITS

AUTHOR/ABBREVIATED ABSTRACT

Since 1970 the National Forests in Oregon and Washington have been operating under a Regionally developed streamside management unit (SMU) concept which is essentially a stream classification system based on use made of the water with specific water quality objectives established for each of the four classes of streams.

Swanson, G.A., tech. coord. 1979. The mitigation symposium: A national workshop on mitigating losses of fish and wildlife habitats. US Dep. Agric. For. Serv. Gen. Tech. Rep. RM-65, 696pp. Rocky Mountain Forest and Range Experiment Station, Fort Collins, CO.

LOCATION: U.S.

KEYWORDS: WETLANDS, MINING, OIL, GAS, HYDROELECTRIC PROJECTS

ABSTRACT

Nine private organizations and eight federal agencies co-sponsored the symposium, which consisted of 133 papers presented in three concurrent sessions (and a poster session) on: coastal zone wetlands; inland wetlands; economic considerations; mining oil, and gas; planning, evaluation, and inventory; surveys; power projects; terrestrial management; aquatic management; legal and political considerations; transportation systems; and state perpspectives.

Sweep, D.H., J.M. Zilincar, B.H. Smith, R.V. Hardy. 1985. Integration of riparian systems management strategies within the context of multiple use land management programs in southwestern Wyoming. Pages 371-373 in Riparian Ecosystems and Their Management: Reconciling Conflicting Uses. Proceedings of the Symposium. US Dep. Agric. For. Serv. Gen. Tech. Rep. RM-120, 523pp. Rocky Mountain Forest and Range Experiment Station, Fort Collins, CO.

LOCATION: WY

KEYWORDS: MULTIPLE USE, RIPARIAN CONDITION

ABSTRACT

The extent of multiple use activities on public lands in southwest Wyoming place significant pressure on riparian ecosystems. Our experience indicates that by using an integrated, interdisciplinary management approach, it is possible to maintain existing healthy riparian habitat, and improve or recover lost habitat.

Swenson, J.E., S.J. Knapp, P.R. Martin, and T.C. Hinz. 1983. Reliability of aerial cache surveys to monitor beaver population trends on prairie rivers in Montana. J. Wildl. Manage. 47(3):697-703.

LOCATION: MT

KEYWORDS: BEAVER, AERIAL CACHE SURVEYS

ABSTRACT

An aerial cache survey was unreliable in indicating population size or trend of beaver (Castor canadensis) on 2 prairie rivers in Montana. Accuracy in locating caches was high (about 90%) and constant among years and areas, but colony size varied among areas and years. Data on age, sex, and reproduction are needed to determine colony size and properly evaluate aerial cache-survey results.

Swenson, E.A. and C.L. Mullins. 1985. Revegetating riparian trees in southwestern floodplains. Pages 135-138 in Riparian Ecosystems and Their Management: Reconciling Conflicting Uses. Proceedings of the Symposium. US Dep. Agric. For. Serv. Gen. Tech. Rep. RM-120, 523pp. Rocky Mountain Forest and Range Experiment Station, Fort Collins, CO.

LOCATION: NM

KEYWORDS: REVEGETATION, COTTONWOOD RIO GRANDE, COTTONWOOD NARROWLEAF, WILLOW GOODING

ABSTRACT

Riparian areas continue to be drastically altered, usually by man's activities. Managers have generally been unsuccessful in using conventional techniques to replace riparian trees. Our experiments with Rio Grande cottonwood, narrowleaf cottonwood, and Gooding willow have shown that a simple and inexpensive method for their reestablishment is now available.

Szaro, R.C., and L.F. DeBano. 1985. The effects of streamflow modification on the development of the riparian ecosystem. Pages 211-213 in Riparian Ecosystems and Their Management: Reconciling Conflicting Uses. Proceedings of the Symposium. US Dep. Agric. For. Serv. Gen. Tech. Rep. RM-120, 523pp. Rocky Mountain Forest and Range Experiment Station, Fort Collins, CO.

LOCATION: AZ

KEYWORDS: FLOOD CONTROL STRUCTURE, EPHEMERAL STREAM DEVELOPMENT

ABSTRACT

The interrelationships between riparian vegetation development and hydrologic regimes in a ephemeral desert stream were examined at Whitlow Ranch Dam along Queen Creek in Pinal County, Arizona. Our data indicates that a flood control structure can have a positive impact on riparian ecosystem development and could be used as a mitigation tool to restore this critically threatened habitat.

Szaro, R.C., S.C. Belfit, and J.N. Rinne. 1985. Impact of grazing on a riparian garter snake. Pages 359-363 in Riparian Ecosystems and Their Management: Reconciling Conflicting Uses. Proceedings of the Symposium. US Dep. Agric. For. Serv. Gen. Tech. Rep. RM-120, 523pp. Rocky Mountain Forest and Range Experiment Station, Fort Collins, CO.

LOCATION: NM

KEYWORDS: GARTER SNAKE, GRAZING IMPACT

ABSTRACT

Numbers of wandering garter snakes (Thamnophis elegans vagrans) were significantly higher where cattle grazing was excluded than along grazed portions of Rio de las Vacas, a high elevation thin-leaf alder - willow riparian community in northern New Mexico. Differences can be attributed to the regeneration of streamside vegetation and the increased amount of organic debris.

Taylor, T.J. and J.S. Barclay. 1985. Renovation of a Plains State Stream--Physical problem solving. Pages 62-66 <u>in</u> Riparian Ecosystems and Their Management: Reconciling Conflicting Uses. Proceedings of the Symposium. US Dep. Agric. For. Serv. Gen. Tech. Rep. RM-120, 523pp. Rocky Mountain Forest and Range Experiment Station, Fort Collins, CO.

LOCATION: OK

KEYWORDS: <u>STREAM IMPROVEMENT</u>

ABSTRACT

Quantifiable methods do not exist to assess hydraulic effects of stream renovation. To obtain such methods, channel obstructions were modeled from field data. These models were used to show changes in flood stages resulting from obstruction removal. This simulation may provide an approach for resource planners to predict flood water control without costly stream channelization.

Thomas, J.W., C. Maser, and J.E. Rodiek. 1979. Riparian zones. Pacific Northwest Forest and Range Experiment Station. US Dep. Agric. For. Serv. Gen. Tech. Rep. PNW-80. 18pp.

LOCATION: OR

KEYWORDS: <u>RIPARIAN HABITAT, WILDLIFE HABITAT</u>

ABSTRACT

Riparian zones are the most critical wildlife habitats in managed rangelands. More wildlife species depend entirely on or spend disproportionately more time in this habitat than any other. The zone is also disproportionately important for grazing, recreation, timber production, fisheries production, road location, and water quality and quantity. The importance to wildlife is examined and guidance given for management.

Thomas, J.W., C. Maser, and J.E. Rodiek. 1979. Riparian Zones. Pages 40-47 in Thomas J.W. ed. Wildlife habitats in managed forests: The Blue Mountains of Oregon and Washington, US Dep. Agric. For. Serv. Agric. Handbook 553. Pacific Northwest Forest and Range Experiment Station, Portland OR. 512pp.

LOCATION: OR

KEYWORDS: TIMBER, GRAZING, RECREATION, WILDLIFE

ABSTRACT

The riparian zone is the most important type of wildlife habitat in the Blue Mountains. It is also the area of maximum potential conflict between users of timber, grazing, recreation, water, and wildlife resources. Riparian zones are usually quite sensitive to management activities and should be cautiously managed. As each riparian zone is somewhat different, the land manager should consult a wildlife biologist and a fishery biologist during the planning process.

Thomas, J.W., C. Maser, and J.E. Rodiek. 1979. Riparian zones in managed rangelands--Their importance to wildlife. Pages 21-31 in Cope, O.B. ed. Grazing and Riparian/Stream Ecosystems: Proceedings of the Forum. Trout Unlimited Inc., Denver, CO. 94pp.

LOCATION: WESTERN U.S.

KEYWORDS: WILDLIFE HABITAT, DISTURBANCE, GRAZING

REVIEWER'S ABSTRACT

Riparian zones: create a well-defined habitat zone within much drier surrounding areas; they make up a minor proportion of the overall area; they are generally more productive in terms of biomass-plant and animal than the remainder of the area; and they are a critical source of diversity within rangelands.

Vanderheyden, J. 1985. Managing multiple resources in Western Cascades forest riparian areas: An example. Pages 448-452 in Riparian Ecosystems and Their Management: Reconciling Conflicting Uses. Proceedings of the Symposium. US Dep. Agric. For. Serv. Gen. Tech. Rep. RM-120, 523pp. Rocky Mountain Forest and Range Experiment Station, Fort Collins, CO.

LOCATION: OR

KEYWORDS: FOREST RIPARIAN AREAS, MULTIPLE USE

ABSTRACT

The USDA Forest Service concepts of multiple use and riparian area dependent resources were incorporated into a district level riparian area management policy. The linkage of riparian areas to the aquatic resource and cumulative watershed processes is integrated into the policy designed to provide consistent direction for on-the-ground management.

Van Haveren, B.P., and W.L. Jackson. 1986. Concepts in stream riparian rehabilitation. Trans. N. Am. Wildl. and Nat. Res. Conf. 51:280-289.

LOCATION: CO

KEYWORDS: RIPARIAN REHABILITATION, WATERSHED MANAGEMENT

AUTHOR/ABBREVIATED ABSTRACT

Stream riparian systems undergoing major geomorphic or hydrologic adjustments should not be treated with habitat improvements until the channel has reached a new dynamic equilibrium. Riparian rehabilitation should not be attempted in stream systems where watershed condition is poor or downward-trending.

Van Velson, R. 1979. Effects of livestock grazing upon rainbow trout in Otter Creek, Nebraska. Pages 53-55 in Cope, O.B. ed. Grazing and Riparian/Stream Ecosystems: Proceedings of the Forum. Trout Unlimited Inc., Denver, CO. 94pp.

LOCATION: NE

KEYWORDS: LIVESTOCK GRAZING, GRAZING IMPACTS, HABITAT RECOVERY, BUFFER ZONE

ABSTRACT

Conditions in Otter Creek exemplified damage improper livestock-management practices can impose on trout. The habitat-improvement project resulted in recovery of the stream and a rebound of the trout population. Results of the project can result when stream habitat receives consideration after improved land-use practices are designed and implemented.

Warner, R.E., and K.M. Hendrix, eds. 1984. California riparian systems. University of California Press, Berkeley, CA 94720. 1035pp.

LOCATION: CA

KEYWORDS: RIVERINE FLOODPLAINS, FORESTS STREAMSIDE, WET MEADOWS, DESERT WASHES, PALM OASIS

ABSTRACT

Proceedings of a conference held in 1981. 128 papers that address major aspects of riparian ecosystems. Subjects of interest to wildlife biologists, fishery biologists, range managers, hydrologists, conservationists, foresters and land managers.

Warren, P.L., and C.R. Schwalbe. 1985. Herpetofauna in riparian habitats along the Colorado River in Grand Canyon. Pages 347-354 in Riparian Ecosystems and Their Management: Reconciling Conflicting Uses. Proceedings of the Symposium. US Dep. Agric. For. Serv. Gen. Tech. Rep. RM-120, 523pp. Rocky Mountain Forest and Range Experiment Station, Fort Collins, CO.

LOCATION: AZ

KEYWORDS: HERPETOFAUNA, RIPARIAN HABITAT

ABSTRACT

Lizard population densities and species composition were sampled in riparian and non-riparian habitats along the Colorado River. The highest densities were found in shoreline habitats, moderate densities in riparian habitats and lowest densities in non-riparian habitats. Rapidly fluctuating river flow levels may have a deleterious effect on lizard populations by trapping populations on alluvial bars and inundating nest sites.

Wesche, T.A., C.M. Goertler, and C.B. Frye. 1985. Importance and evaluation of instream and riparian cover in smaller trout streams. Pages 325-328 in Riparian Ecosystems and Their Management: Reconciling Conflicting Uses. Proceedings of the Symposium. US Dep. Agric. For. Serv. Gen. Tech. Rep. RM-120, 523pp. Rocky Mountain Forest and Range Experiment Station, Fort Collins, CO.

LOCATION: WY

KEYWORDS: RIPARIAN COVER, TROUT STREAMS

ABSTRACT

Cover is an important trout habitat component resulting from the geomorphological characteristics of a stream channel, the streambank interface with the riparian community, and the streamflow. This paper quantitatively describes the significance of the riparian contribution to overall stream cover as related to brown trout population size.

Willoughby, J.W., and W. Davilla. 1984. Plant species composition and life form spectra of tidal streambanks and adjacent riparian woodlands along the lower Sacramento River. Pages 642-647 in California Riparian Systems: Ecology, Conservation, and Productive Management, Warner, R.E. and K. Hendrix eds. 1035pp. University of California Press, Berkeley, CA.

LOCATION: CA

KEYWORDS: STREAMBANKS TIDAL, RIPARIAN WOODLAND PLANT SPECIES

ABSTRACT

Flora and life forms of the tidal streambank plant community along the Sacramento River near Collinsville, Solano County, California are compared to those of adjacent plant communities. The tidal streambank flora has a significantly smaller non-native component than the floras of adjacent riparian woodland and annual grassland communities. All three communities have developed in historically disturbed habitats. Rhizomatous herbs represent the predominant life form of the tidal streambank community. In contrast, the riparian woodland community has a much lower percentage of rhizomatous herbs and higher percentages of annual and woody species. Reasons for these differences are discussed.

York, J.C. 1985. Dormant stub planting techniques. Pages 513-514 in Riparian Ecosystems and Their Management: Reconciling Conflicting Uses. Proceedings of the Symposium. US Dep. Agric. For. Serv. Gen. Tech. Rep. RM-120, 523pp. Rocky Mountain Forest and Range Experiment Station, Fort Collins, CO.

LOCATION: AZ

KEYWORDS: STREAMBANK STABILAZTION, TREE PLANTING, STREAM CHANNEL EROSION

ABSTRACT

Bank and levee stabilization was done by using dormant stubs of black willow and cottonwood along the toes of banks and levees. 3-6 inch logs, 6-7 feet long, planted into the water table, resulted in exceptionally good survival and first season growth. The original 2,000 feet of plantings have survived 3 minor and 1 major flood and have given survival to the levee they protect.

Youngblood, A.P., W.G. Pagett, and A.H. Winward. 1985. Riparian
community type classification in the Intermountain Region. Pages
510-512 in Riparian Ecosystems and Their Management: Reconciling
Conflicting Uses. Proceedings of the Symposium. US Dep. Agric. For.
Serv. Gen. Tech. Rep. RM-120, 523pp. Rocky Mountain Forest and Range
Experiment Station, Fort Collins, CO.

LOCATION: ID, UT, WY

KEYWORDS: CLASSIFICATION

ABSTRACT

Classification of riparian ecosystems in Idaho, Wyoming, and Utah
into different community types, based upon similarities in floristic
composition, provides a tool for resource management. Diagnostic
keys that utilize conspicuous plant species provide for field
identification. Environmental relationships, successional status,
and management implications are discussed.

INDEX